SO YOU WANT TO BE
A MAGICIAN

Have you ever watched a magician and wished you could do some of his tricks? This book lets you into the secrets and tells you about the basic types of magic, including, comedy, 'appearance', 'vanishes', 'transformations' and 'restorations'. There are some tricks for each kind, details of how they work and all you need for your first steps in magic.

LAURENCE B. WHITE Jnr.

So you want to be a Magician?

Illustrated by Bill Morrison

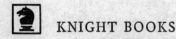
KNIGHT BOOKS
in association with SCHOLASTIC PUBLICATIONS

To Sarge Desmond, 'The Whiz of a Wizard', and his
three greatest tricks . . . Nancy, Martha and Rachel.

ISBN 0 340 18508 2

This edition published 1974 by Knight, the paperback
division of Brockhampton Press, Leicester.
First published in 1972 by Addison–Wesley Publishing
Company Inc. Reading, Massachusetts, U.S.A.
Revised edition

Printed and bound in Great Britain by
Cox & Wyman Ltd, London, Reading and Fakenham

CONTENTS

CHAPTER 1

SO YOU WANT TO BE A MAGICIAN?

So you want to be a magician? Do you really know what you are asking? Do you really know what a magician is or what he does?

Many people think he is just a person who pulls rabbits from empty hats, makes beautiful ladies float in the air, or cuts people in half without hurting them. A magician is really much more.

If you read a dictionary definition you might find that he is a person who 'produces effects using supernatural assistants or secret forces of nature'. This is a very ancient idea and a magician really can't do these things.

He is a person who can appear to do the impossible. Most people, for example, cannot produce a real handkerchief from an empty box. The person who can appear to do impossible things is called a magician.

You can't learn, or be taught, to do real magic simply because there is no such thing. You can't really find a handkerchief in an empty box any more than you can really create secret spells or conjure up demons. If you want to be a magician you may be disappointed to learn that there is no book that can ever teach you this. But if you want to learn how to *act* like a magician, that is a different story, and that is just what this book is all about.

Probably the best definition of a modern magician came from Robert-Houdin, a stage magician who lived about 100 years ago. He said that a magician is really only 'an actor playing the part of a magician'.

If you would like to learn to act like one you will find many ideas here to help you. This means that you must learn much more than just how the tricks are done ... you must learn to be a good actor. And this takes hard work. But if you have ever longed to be an actor who could stand before an audience and convince the spectators that what they were seeing was actually happening, then perhaps you are the right person to become a magician.

TOOLS OF YOUR TRADE

A person who knows a lot of tricks is not a magician! A trick is just one tool of a magician's trade much like a hammer is just one tool of a carpenter's. The carpenter couldn't build a house without his hammer, but the hammer alone cannot build a house either. Building a house requires a great many tools, plus knowledge and skill. Knowing how a trick is done is only one tiny part of learning to be a magician. The tricks themselves are actually a very small secret. The magician's biggest secret is knowing how to convince people that he is indeed a magician. If you want to become a magician you not only want to learn what he does, but you must also learn what he is. A magician is an actor.

WHAT IS A MAGIC TRICK?

Many people pick up magic books and thumb through them, stopping here and there to study a trick. These people don't really want to be magicians, they just want to know how a magician does his tricks.

Usually they are disappointed because the tricks are very simple. Even when they appear to defy a science rule they usually work by using some other science principle.

Magic tricks are simply clever puzzles. If they are presented just as a puzzle they are easily figured out. When a magician acts the puzzle out as something that is 'really' magic, however, he can usually confuse anyone.

Here is a trick I would like to do for you right now. Please do the arithmetic that follows before you read further!

1 Write down any three digit number (each numeral to be different).
2 Reverse the numbers and if the new number is larger than the original, write it above the original, if smaller write it below.
3 Subtract the smaller from the larger number.
4 Reverse the numbers in the subtraction total and ADD this new number and the subtraction total together.
5 ADD together all of the separate numbers in your final total.

Now, here is the surprise. Before you started to do the arithmetic, I wrote this book, right? And, therefore, I must be a magician if I wrote that your final total would be

18

Of course, you will quickly say that magic had nothing to do with it, but it was a trick with numbers and a simple experiment with mathematics. You, of course, are quite correct.

How it happens is simply a puzzle. If you are good with your arithmetic you may be able to figure it out. More important though, if you are a good actor you can use this exact same puzzle to convince your audience that you must be a real magician. You'll learn how to do this later on. So a magician is an actor who can take puzzles and make them appear to be miracles, and this is what you really want to learn. You'll find this is much more fun than just knowing the secret of how the tricks work. It's like learning how to build a house instead of just learning how to use a hammer!

CHAPTER 2

COMEDY MAGIC – TRICKS TO LAUGH AT

In the world we live, it is probably impossible actually to convince anyone that a magician has any strange or mysterious powers. Most people know a trick or two themselves and they fully realize that anything you do is simply another puzzle they cannot immediately explain.

Why do people enjoy watching a magician? There are many reasons. They like to be challenged. They like to use their brains. They enjoy imagining, just for a moment, that science can be defied. Most important of all though is that people like to be entertained.

This is your biggest job as a magician. It is the actor's job to entertain his audience, and you are just one special kind of actor.

One of the easiest ways for a beginner to be a good entertaining actor is to include several good comedy magic tricks in his programme. When people are laughing you know they are being entertained.

Actually, any trick can be performed in a funny way. Often a serious trick can be made funny with some funny talk. A magician calls his talk *patter*. Patter can be just an occasional line which makes people chuckle, for example:

'To do this trick I must use a special piece of rope. It must have a centre exactly in the middle and not more than two ends.

'I'm going to cut this rope with this pair of shizzors. I say shizzors because I've never been able to say scissors.

'Do you know how to get a piece of rope with only one end? All you have to do is find a piece with two ends and cut one off.

'I'm going to use some water for this trick. You know what water is don't you? It's that clear liquid that gets dirty when you wash it.'

Sometimes a 'play on words' will indicate that the trick is all in fun. Here are a few you might try:

'My next trick is simply awful ... er, I mean awfully simple.

'Some magician's are good, and some are lousy. Today you will see a little of both ... because I am good and lousy!

'Shall we do another trick? Well as one magic rabbit said to another ... let-us.'

You will find many little jokes, riddles, plays on words, or funny stories you can use with your magic. Collect all you can. Remember, knowing how the trick works does not make you a magician; knowing how to use the tricks to *entertain* does! The best magicians spend more time working out what to say during the trick than they spend practising the trick itself.

Some professional magicians perform their acts without saying a single word. Most young magicians, however, will find their audience becomes bored with this. A young audience prefers to laugh, be noisy, and have a good time ... they simply won't sit still long enough for you to play Mr Mysterious.

Your patter can consist of a series of short *one-liner* type jokes like those listed above, or you might develop a long 'tall story' to describe your trick. You might, for example, tell how you travelled deep into the boon-docks of India and found an ancient bearded Hindu sleeping on a bed of nails. When he awoke from his hypnotic trance he gave you this small mysterious ruby red sphere and instructed you how to chant the mystical incantation that would ... and so forth!

Even if the story is not funny by itself, the longer and more complicated it sounds the louder your audience will laugh. An absolutely incredible lie can be very, very entertaining.

Some tricks, you will find, are funny because of what happens in them. In this case you do not have to say much of anything funny, but you must still be a convincing actor. Here are two funny tricks you can try.

MAGIC BY THE BOOK

On the table is a paper cup and a pitcher containing a little water. The magician borrows a felt hat from a man in the audience.

'I've never tried this trick before, but I would like to show it to you anyway. Now let's see, first I put the hat on the table. Then I put the cup in the hat (he does so). No, no, that's not right (he takes the cup out and places it back on he table) first I put the hat on the table ... Oh, I already did that. Ah ... then I pour the water into the hat.'

He picks up the pitcher and pours the water into the hat. The cup is still lying on the table. The audience begins to laugh at the magician's confusion.

'Now I take the cup and ... oh my goodness, I've done something wrong. Let me see.'

The magician picks up a magic book, opens it and reads a few words aloud. Then to the audience he says: 'Oh yes, you put the hat on the table. I've already done that. Then place the cup into the hat. (He does this.) Then you remove the cup from the hat, and pour the water into the pitcher.'

He takes the cup right back out of the hat and, sure enough it has filled with water which is poured out. Still reading, the magician says, 'Then return the hat to the gentleman who loaned it.' He sets the book aside and hands back the empty *and dry* hat saying. 'I knew I should have read those directions again before trying to show you that trick!'

HOW TO DO IT: Naturally your audience will laugh. You appear to do everything wrong and this is precisely why the trick works so well. Of course you do not actually bumble your way through it. You require some preparation and plenty of practice.

You will require one hat, one pitcher containing about a half a cupful of water, a magic book (how about this one?) and *two* paper cups.

The two paper cups should both be the same size and should slip easily inside one another. Cut the rim off one of the cups and cut a large hole in the bottom of the other. Drop the one with the hole inside the rim-less one. From a short distance they will appear as a single cup.

To perform the trick turn the hat upside-down and place it on the table. Using two hands place the cup(s) inside. Following the patter story you then remove the cup again, but actually remove only the inner bottomless cup, tipping is so the audience can't see the bottom and leave the plain one in the hat. Be sure the cup remaining in the hat stays upright.

Set the bottomless cup down on the table beside the hat.

Next you pour water into the 'empty' hat. Actually the water is poured very carefully into the cup hidden inside.

After 'reading' your book you pick up the bottomless cup. Set this cup slowly back down inside the hat. Be sure it goes into the one already there, and push it down well so the two cups will again appear as one.

You are now ready to remove the cup from the hat, pour out the water, and return the hat empty and dry.

If you can't easily borrow a hat, or don't want to bother, you can use one of your own. Begin with the hat on your head and, at the end, read the directions from the book as, 'Then place the hat back on your head.' Your audience will still expect you to get wet, so they will be fully as surprised.

WHAT IS BRAND X?

A pitcher of clear water, five empty glasses and a small bottle of fluid marked BRAND X resting on the table. The magician begins to tell his story:

'We have all seen many television commercials which use a Brand X, or secret ingredient. So I felt you might enjoy seeing a real live demonstration of this magical X stuff,' explains the magician.

'Actually I should begin by explaining that I have worked for many years for a company that manufactures soda pop. It's called *Bug Juice, the Warmer Cola.* Originally we called it *Crystal Clear, the Warmer Cola* but we discovered that people just wouldn't buy more than one bottle. It seems that every time it was poured it changed to red!'

The magician pours some of the clear water from the pitcher into the first glass. It changes to a bright red colour.

'Every glass mysteriously changed to red.'

He pours out another glass which also turns red. Picking

up the two red glasses he pours them into the water in the pitcher and all the water becomes red.

'Even if the cola was poured back to where it came from it stayed the same . . . it even changed the rest of the Crystal Clear Cola red.

'Now you see the problem that faced my company. They certainly couldn't call it *Red Cola* because it didn't look red when you bought it, and, anyway, everybody knows that fire engines may be red . . . even books may be read . . . but cola is never red! Now let me get back to my original demonstration showing the importance of Brand X. When Brand X was discovered, our problems were easily solved. When we added Brand X to our cola it became Crystal Clear again . . . which is naturally why we re-named it Bug Juice.'

While explaining the above, the magician has poured some of the fluid from the Brand X bottle into the pitcher of red water. He stirs it a bit with a spoon and it turns perfectly clear once again.

'Now,' he explains, 'we were right back in business. Right back from where we started. Thanks to that wonderful Brand X ingredient we never again had anyone complain about our cola turning red when it was poured into a glass!'

As he says this, the magician pours the water into the three glasses remaining on the table . . . the clear water changes to green, yellow, and blue!

HOW TO DO IT: This is a chemical trick. Your audience will probably guess that the instant the first glass of liquid turns the water red. Remember that you are not really trying to mystify them with this trick, you are simply trying to entertain them and make them laugh. You even admit that you are using chemicals when you add Brand X, but the final unexpected surprise of three different colours at the end will make them aware of your magical 'powers'.

The chemicals you will use are easy to obtain. Your mother

will probably have them all and, if she doesn't, you can purchase them at any handy grocery store. Obtain some *food colouring*. These are small bottles of very concentrated coloured chemicals. They are used to give colour to such things as cake icing, so they are perfectly harmless to use. You will require four different colours, red, green, yellow and blue. You will also need a little *liquid laundry bleach*. You can handle this with complete safety, however, do not spill it on your clothing (it may take the colour out!) and, certainly don't put it in your mouth.

To set up this trick place five clear glasses in a row on the table. Before your audience arrives, place a couple of drops (you won't need more!) of red food colouring in the first two glasses. In the last three glasses place a couple of drops of the other colours: green in one, yellow in another, and blue in the last. By using just a couple of drops of this very concentrated colouring your audience will not notice them resting on the bottom.

Next, fill a *clear* pitcher with plain water and set it down on the table beside the row of glasses.

Now obtain a small bottle, the fancier-looking the better. Make a label for the bottle that reads BRAND X, in big dark letters. Fill the bottle with liquid laundry bleach and set this on the table. You will also need a spoon to stir with and you're ready to go.

By reading the above patter story, and doing what the magician did you will readily understand how the trick is done. First, the water is poured into the two glasses with the drops of red food colouring. The water turns red. Next these two glasses are poured back into the pitcher which turns all the water red. Brand-X is added next, give a stir and the pitcher of water will become colourless. You do not have to use much bleach for this. The red colour will 'bleach out' easily and this will surprise your audience even more.

Surprisingly, a little bleach will not bleach out green, yellow, or blue food colours quickly. So when you pour the same water into the last three glasses they will change to these colours. (Note: the bleach will affect the colours after a while, so when the trick is done move them out of sight.)

PLEASE: *Do not drink the water after you add the bleach!* Bleach is a poison if swallowed and could make you quite sick. Pour it down a sink just to be sure nobody in the audience decides to try it either. Also, be sure to wash your glasses and pitcher after doing this trick. If they're not perfectly clean the bleach that's left may prevent the trick from working well the next time you try it.

Try making up another story using this trick. Maybe you could be a TV announcer showing how wonderful your new 'Household Bleach' is (by adding it to some red water) but becoming confused later and having unexpected colours appearing suddenly. How about a magician who tries to do the famous *Wine To Water* trick, but says the wrong 'magic words' and gets wrong colours? This is a good way to make up your own story. You might find that making up stories is as much fun as performing the trick. Also magicians usually find it is easier to tell their own stories rather than trying to tell someone else's!

Another kind of comedy that is very useful to a magic show is simply called a *bit of business*. This is just something silly that makes people laugh and amuses them between real magic tricks. Sometimes these can be used at parties, sometimes when you meet a friend on the street. Often magicians like them in a real show to give their audience more variety. They might be called a 'change of pace' trick.

For example, try this on a friend.

IT'S A DATE

Here's a chance to act very mysterious, and end up being very foolish at the same time. Offer your friend a handful of pennies and invite him to choose any one he likes. Ask him to look at the date and remember it.

'Would you be amazed, and think I was the best magician in the world if I could tell you the date?' His answer will probably be 'Yes'.

Think about it for a while. Concentrate very hard. Make him wonder if you are actually 'reading his mind'. Finally, in your most magical voice announce:

'The date . . . the date . . . is . . . (whatever today's date is). All I promised to do was tell you the date, and you have to be honest and admit I did it didn't I?'

Often when you invite a member of the audience up to assist you with a trick you can work a bit of business with him. The audience enjoys this and it is fun for you too. Here is an example of something you might try when you first invite a helper up to the stage.

AN EGG-STRA TRICK

A helper is invited up from the audience to assist with some trick. As he approaches, the magician says 'Hello' and extends his hand for a handshake. Just as the helper's hand touches his, the magician pulls his own away and turns it up to show an egg in it.

'What were you doing with this egg?'

The audience laughs. The boy says he didn't bring the egg, but the magician keeps right on talking.

'Were you going to throw this egg at me if my tricks were no good? Yes, I'll bet that's why you brought it. But I caught you didn't I?'

After fooling with his helper a few moments the magician then asks the audience: 'Well he certainly won't be needing this egg while he's up here with me. In fact, I wouldn't trust him with it. Would anybody out there like it?'

Someone asks for the egg. 'Here,' says the magician throwing the egg towards the audience.

The audience will probably try to duck, but instead of

being showered with messy egg, coloured confetti will fall over them. The egg has vanished.

HOW TO DO IT: First you must 'blow' a hen's egg. This is easily done by using a sewing needle carefully to prick a hole about ¼ inch in diameter through the shell at each end of the egg. By being careful and beginning with small holes and enlarging them you can do this easily. Next take a small piece of wire and push it into one of the holes. Wiggle it around inside the egg to break up the yolk. Hold the egg over a small dish with one hole pointing down over it. Blow hard into the other hole and the inside of the egg will spill out the opposite hole into the dish. Your mother can still use the egg for cooking, so don't throw it away.

Set the egg shell aside for a day or so, until the inside is completely dry. When it's dry, paste a small piece of paper over one of the holes.

Cut some coloured paper into tiny bits to use for your confetti. A page from a comic book will make fine confetti. Fill the inside of the eggshell with this confetti, and paste another piece of paper over the open hole in the eggshell to seal it shut.

Place this egg in your right hand coat pocket. During your show, invite someone up to help you. If you are right handed, arrange it so that he approaches you to your left, or ask him to step up to your left. As he approaches, reach into your pocket and remove the egg with your right hand. Drop your hand down by your side and turn it so the audience doesn't notice the egg. Remember, nobody knows you are beginning a trick, so nobody will be watching you very carefully.

As your helper approaches, extend the hand holding the egg out towards him. Since he is on your left, your right hand will hide the egg. Hold the egg under your thumb, palm down and fingers out. He will reach out with his hand, because it looks as though you want to shake. Just as his hand touches yours, pull your hand back turn it over and let the audience see the egg.

Next you will ask if anyone in the audience wants the egg. It will probably surprise you to discover that quite a number will shout 'Yes!' and hold up their hands. I've never been able to figure out what they intend to do with it, but you can be sure someone will always want it. As you toss it towards the audience, give the egg a hard squeeze. The dry eggshell will break into dozens of pieces and mix with the confetti which showers down on the people towards the front.

Still another bit of business you might try with a helper gives you something to do with him *after* he has helped you with a trick. It also gives him a souvenir which he can keep and take home to show his friends.

THE MAGICIAN WILL MAKE YOU A STAR

As he invites a helper up to assist him with a trick, the magician makes a promise.

'I would like to have someone to help me who has always wanted to be in show business. Someone who has always dreamed of being a big star. I promise that I will make whoever helps me a star today.'

After the helper is selected, and used in the trick, the magician picks up a square of paper and a pair of scissors. Without saying anything, he proceeds to fold the paper into a small package and cuts it into two pieces with the scissors. He hands the bigger piece to his helper and keeps the smaller one for himself.

'Would you open your paper please,' he asks.

The helper opens the bundle and discovers the paper is cut in the shape of a large star.

'I promised you that if you assisted me with my magic trick I would make you a star,' explains the magician, 'in fact, I've even done better than that. I've made you two of them!'

He opens the sheet he is holding and it is the large cut out of the same star. He hands the paper to his helper and lets him return to his seat.

HOW TO DO IT: There is no magic here, just a bit of practice in paper-folding and cutting. The illustrations will show you how to do it. Begin with a piece of paper about 8½ inches square which is cut from a sheet of writing paper. Later you can use a bigger piece for your shows, like a piece of squared-off newspaper. Any *perfectly square* piece of paper can be used.

1 First fold the paper in half.

2 Next fold the bottom of the folded paper up so it touches the top edge about a quarter of the way in from the right side.

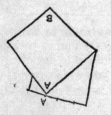

3 Then fold the lower right corner up even with the diagonal fold.

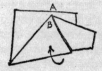

21

4 Finally fold the upper left corner down so it is even with the right edge.

5 With the scissors, cut the paper as shown, right on the dotted line.

6 Open up both papers and you will find:

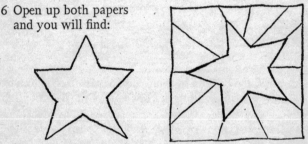

Naturally you can have the folds already in the paper which will allow you to do this quickly during your performance. You can also pencil in the line to cut along to make the best star. In experimenting you will learn that the angle you cut the folded paper on is very important in making the shape of the final star. It is worth practising.

Very little of this section has taught you any tricks that seem really magical. And yet it is one of the most important sections in this whole book. It reminds us that learning tricks is simply not enough; you must learn to be an entertainer. Comedy is one of the most important tools a young magician should learn to use. After all everyone expects a magic show to be lots of *fun* and it can be.

CHAPTER 3

MIS-DIRECTION – IT'S WHERE YOU LOOK

The magician is standing to one side of the stage. He holds a large cloth and shows that it is empty on both sides. 'Now watch,' he says, then he calls to an assistant, 'Bring me a basket.' A pretty girl walks on to the other side of the stage carrying a large basket. She walks towards the waiting magician and suddenly she trips and falls. The basket clatters around on the stage. The girl is obviously embarrassed, but she gets up, retrieves the basket, and walks to the magician.

The audience is still laughing at her clumsiness; but wait, the magician has gathered the cloth into a ball and something is moving about under it. Slowly he removes the cloth and discloses a very large live duck. He places the duck in the basket and the girl walks offstage with it.

Can you guess how the magician got the duck?

Think of the order in which things happened, and where they happened. The magician was showing his cloth close to one side of the stage. *After* he showed the empty cloth to the audience, he called for the girl. The audience glanced slightly to the other side of the stage and watched her come on, but they still watched the magician closely, too. Suddenly the girl tripped and what happened then? Every person turned to see what had happened. In that moment, while all eyes were off him, the magician simply reached offstage and was handed a duck by another assistant. He quickly hid this duck behind the cloth. The girl picked herself up and walked towards the magician. By now everyone's eyes had returned to him, but it was too late! He was already gathering up the cloth. When he uncovered the live duck, everyone was astonished. Probably they applauded him for doing a great trick! But who really did the trick? The silly, clumsy-footed girl who stumbled and fell at just the right moment. The girl provided the magician with his *mis-direction*.

Mis-direction is a big word that is of great importance to every magician. Probably more than half of any magician's tricks require the use of mis-direction. What is mis-direction? It is making the audience look the right way at the wrong time, the wrong way at the right time, or simply making the audience look where *you* want it to look and not where it should be looking.

Imagine how simple it would be to make things appear or vanish if your audience would simply shut its eyes when you wanted it to. Mis-direction allows you to do almost the same thing except they can keep their eyes open.

Please do not try to perform the *Appearing-Duck* trick used as an example above. This is a trick that belongs to a professional stage magician with many years of practice. It requires split-second timing and much experience to know just when to reach for the duck. Learning to make people look where you want requires much practice on your part. It will probably take many 'tries' before you will really believe it is possible. You will be wise to try some simple tricks using mis-direction for just one or two friends at a time. As your skill and confidence grow, you will find many more complicated tricks that will challenge your mis-directional skills.

Here are four basic rules of mis-direction:

People will look . . .
. . . Where you *look*
. . . Where you *point*
. . . Where there is a *sudden noise*.
. . . Where something *happens*

Often a magic trick will use several of these principles at the same time. For example, if you say to a friend, 'look',

24

and you point and look towards the ceiling, he will look there also. But try saying, 'look' and *pointing* up to the ceiling while *looking* down towards the floor at the same time. I'll bet your friend will be very puzzled and will not know where he should look. If you want your friend to 'see' an imaginary object, you must both look, and point at it just as though you, too, actually see it!

Would you like to see how easy it is to make your friend look where you want? Here's a quick trick to try. It probably won't fool anybody for more than a moment, but, if you practice it you'll be amazed at how easy it is to fool a friend with mis-direction.

DISSOLVING BALL

The magician holds a small ball in his hands. He tosses it up into the air a few times. On a final throw, the ball seems to vanish into thin air.

HOW TO DO IT: Hold a small ball (even a crumpled paper ball will do) between the palms of your hands. Hold your palms together as though you were saying your prayers. *Stand sideways* to your friend so that he sees the back of one of your hands. Now, *look* at your hands. Toss the ball up into the air and *watch* the ball go up and back down to your hands. Repeat this several times. Be sure to begin each throw with your hands held in the praying position with the ball inside.

Finally move your hands up quickly as though you threw the ball, but actually keep your palms together with the ball held inside. Be sure to 'watch the ball' ... that is, the path the ball would have taken. Your friend, following your eyes, will look into empty air and discover that the ball is not there. If your mis-direction is good your friend will be momentarily amazed.

If you practice this simple trick long enough, and toss the

ball high enough, you may discover that you actually have enough time ... while your friend's eyes are following the path of the imaginary ball ... to drop the real ball into your pocket. If you do this quickly, and then return your hands to their original position, you will be able to show that your hands are empty and prove that the ball did vanish.

This trick is real magic. It will not work itself. You must make your friend look at the wrong place at the right time. When you are able to do this you are well on your way to becoming a real magician and this kind of magic will fool any of your friends who happen to know a few tricks also. Remember, anyone can do tricks ... but it takes real skill to do magic!

This first trick with mis-direction is a perfect example of the *where-you-look* rule. Most beginners fail with this trick because they look where the ball really is and not where it is supposed to be. It reminds us that a magician really has to think about what he is doing. Fooling people is hard work and requires a great amount of concentration.

Looking is almost always an important part of mis-direction but other things can help you also. For more practice here is a trick that uses the rule of *where-you-point*. Remember to look where you point for double mis-direction.

A ROLLING STRAW

Placing a short piece of drinking straw on the table the magician suggests that everyone should, 'Watch the straw very carefully.'

He rests his pointing finger on the table so that it is pointing at one end of the straw. Slowly he moves his finger down the table. Nothing happens. He returns his finger to the end of the straw and repeats the action. Again nothing happens. On the next try however, the straw suddenly begins to roll, all by itself, down the table beside his finger. The magician picks up the straw and returns it to its original position.

Again, without touching it in any way, his finger seems to attract the straw and causes it to roll down the table.

HOW TO DO IT: You will need only a paper or plastic drinking straw. In fact, if you cut it in half and use only one half you will find the trick easier to perform.

It is important that the table, straw, you, and your friend be in the right positions. Your friend should be beside you, and should not watch from the other side of the table. You don't want him to feel your breath as you blow on the straw.

Bend your head down so that your face is about one foot away from the straw. Point your forefinger at one end of the straw. Be sure that the straw is several inches away from the end of your finger so your friend will realize that you are not simply trying to push it.

His eyes will be attracted towards the straw by your pointing finger. Again, for perfect mis-direction, be sure to keep *your* eyes intently glued on that straw. Your fingers, your words, and your eyes must insist that your friend watch that straw carefully!

Now draw your finger down the table beside the straw. Nothing is going to happen, but be an actor and convince your friend that something *is* going to happen and he shouldn't miss it.

The third time you draw your finger down the table open your lips and blow on the straw. Your breath should be so gentle that your friend doesn't hear it, but strong enough to cause the straw to roll. However fast it rolls you will find you can always move your finger along with it. You will see how easily your audience is fooled into believing that some mysterious force emanating from your finger is responsible.

The trick is simple. It sounds almost too simple to actually fool anybody, but if you practice your mis-direction well you may find your friend explaining what happened by 'static electricity' or 'vibrations in the table'. Let him guess what he might, but you know that you have just scored another point in making people look where *you* want.

Would you like to change a penny into two pence? Of course without any real magic to aid you, you will have to provide both the penny and the two pence. But you can achieve this surprising effect by using a bit of mis-direction that depends on the rule of *a sudden noise*. Again, it is important that you remember to look the right way, too.

THE PENNY KEEPS GETTING BIGGER

'Would you like to see me make a penny vanish?'

The magician shows a penny in his right hand. He bends his left arm so his left hand rests against his shoulder. He presses the penny against his left elbow. With the palm of his right hand he starts to rub it vigorously against the elbow.

'I'm afraid I can't do it,' he says, 'Instead of getting smaller this penny just seems to get bigger!'

Opening his hand the magician discovers two pence. The penny is completely gone.

HOW TO DO IT: Put a two pence piece and a penny in your right trousers pocket. To begin the trick remove the penny and two pence in your right hand. Hold the two pence hidden in your closed fist and show the penny held between your first two fingers and thumb. Begin to rub the penny against your left elbow as described above.

As you are rubbing 'accidentally' allow the penny to slip from your fingers and fall to the floor. This is the first bit of mis-direction. Everyone will be attracted to the sound of the coin hitting the floor. Be sure you look at it too.

Now, and read this carefully, reach to the floor and pick up the penny with your *left* hand (you'll have to take your hand off your shoulder to do this).

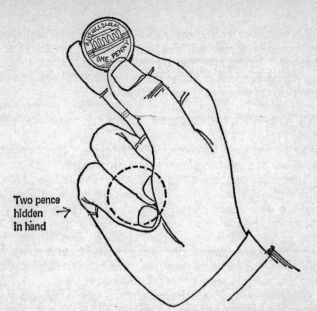

Two pence
hidden
in hand →

Now, naturally, to continue with the trick you must return it to your right hand. Put your two hands together as though you were transferring the penny, but actually you do not change it at all. Keep the coin hidden in your left hand.

Hold the right hand, back to the audience, as though it now held the penny (remember, it still holds the two pence). Return your left hand to your shoulder and begin rubbing the 'penny' into your elbow once again. While you are doing this, keep looking at your elbow as you simply drop the real penny in your left hand down your collar inside your shirt. The mis-direction provided by your elbow rubbing will enable you to do this completely unnoticed. You are then left with the two pence in your right hand which allows you to finish the trick without any trace of what happened to the penny.

Thus far, because of your looking, pointing or making a

noise, you have learned tricks that have made your audience look where you wanted them to. There is one last mis-direction rule you should investigate: people will *look where something happens*. You can use this principle to get rid of a coin *after* you appear to make it vanish.

THE GREAT JAIL ESCAPE

After borrowing a handkerchief and a penny, the magician sits down at a table and begins to tell this story:

'Magicians sometimes allow themselves to be locked into handcuffs, chains, or even jail cells, and, quick as a wink make a miraculous escape. These kinds of magicians call themselves escape artists and I would like to show you how they go about their tricks. I would like to demonstrate the most famous escape of all ... the escape from a blanket! Let's imagine for a moment that this handkerchief is the blanket, and this penny is the escape artist ...'

The magician spreads the hankerchief on the tabletop and places the penny on top, in the middle.

'First we must lock the magician securely inside the blanket. We do it in this way ...' He rolls the handkerchief around the penny and then ties the handkerchief into a tight knot.

'The magician is now trapped securely inside this escape-proof cell ... but watch ... one, two, three. The magician has escaped right before your eyes.'

He tossed the handkerchief, still knotted, on to the table and invites the owner to open the knot. When it is done it is found that the penny has not only escaped but has completely disappeared. When the magician is asked where the penny is, he simply answers:

'I'm sorry, I told you I would demonstrate how escape artists work. I did not say that I knew how they did it!'

HOW TO DO IT: Sit at a table so that your lap is directly

under the edge of the tabletop. Spread a handkerchief diagonally away from you, so that one corner is hanging over
the edge of the table and directly over your lap. Lay a penny
in the centre of the handkerchief.

Fold the corner of the handkerchief furthest from you
over the penny so that this corner also hangs over the edge
of the table.

Now, pretend to grasp the penny through the centre of
the folded handkerchief, but actually leave the penny free
and just squeeze the cloth. Pick the handkerchief up and off
the table. If you do this properly the last corners to
come off the table will be those hanging over the edge. As
you lift the handkerchief, the penny will slip down and
finally, just before you lift it completely away from the
table, the penny will fall into your lap. Nobody will see this
because the action is hidden by the cloth, and they feel you
are holding the penny in the centre of the handkerchief.

Once off the table, immediately lay the handkerchief
down once again . . . this time in the centre of the table.

Now begin to roll the handkerchief into a tube. Once this
is done, quickly tie the tube into a tight knot. Be sure to pull
the knot tight. The audience should be convinced that the
penny is securely inside that knot.

Lift the knotted handkerchief, with your left hand, above
the tabletop. Keep your eyes on it and everyone else will
also (mis-direction!). Lower your right hand to your lap and
pick up the penny, but keep your hand on your lap.

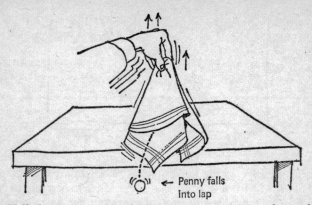

Penny falls
into lap

Talk for a moment and count one, two, three and toss the handkerchief towards its owner.

What will happen now? Your friend will be anxious to see if the penny is still in the handkerchief. So will everybody else. Your friend will struggle to open the knot. Everybody will be watching him. Their eyes (and your eyes too, please) will be on that knot ... that's where something is happening! This is the mis-direction you require: without taking your eyes off the knotted handkerchief, simply raise your right hand and drop the hidden penny into your pocket. The trick is done for you. You may sit back, relax, and wait for your audience to be amazed!

From this, and other tricks with mis-direction, you have learned that it is most important to look where you want your audience to look. This is a rule that must be practised by all magicians. You will discover how important your eyes and motions are in showing people what you want. You will have to be a good actor, and you will remember from Chapter 1 that a magician is just an actor, playing the part of a magician. The actor uses his words, actions, and his eyes to convince his audience that he is truly the person he claims to be. Learning to use good mis-direction is simply a big step forward in learning to be a good actor.

CHAPTER 4

FORCING – MAKING THE CHOICE RIGHT

Picking up a deck of playing cards, the magician begins plucking cards off the top one by one. 'Stop me any time you wish,' he invites his audience.

After a few more cards have been dealt, someone shouts, 'Stop!' The magician walks forward and has him pick the card off the top of the deck and asks the spectator (who will also be his helper) to show everyone the card he has chosen.

The magician tears the card into small pieces and drops them into an envelope. He removes one torn corner and hands it to the spectator to hold. The envelope is sealed and placed in his shirt pocket, poking out in plain view.

On the table is a dish containing four oranges. The spectator is invited to choose one of them. The magician removes the envelope from his pocket, holds it over the orange and gives it a shake. He hands the envelope to the spectator to open. The pieces of the card are gone.

Handing a knife to the helper, the magician suggests that he cut the orange in half. Inside the opened orange the spectator finds a rolled up card. It is the same one originally chosen, but it is completely whole . . . except for one small torn off corner that is missing. The spectator tries to fit the piece he was given earlier to hold into the space. It matches exactly!

Is this real magic? Not at all. It is simply a very fine example of a trick using the magician's tool he calls a *force*. It is one of his most powerful secrets.

You can do this same kind of trick, but it won't work itself. You will have to work hard, have lots of nerve, and make it happen. You will learn how this orange trick works just a bit later, but you are much wiser in learning about forcing first.

Forcing is just what the word sounds like ... forcing, or *making* a person do something he would rather not do. In a magician's case this is doubly difficult because you must make a person choose what you want him to, not necessarily what he wishes to, and yet *he must always feel that the choice was his*. He must not feel that he was forced in any way, but that he was completely free to make his own selection.

Magicians have devised many ways to do this. Some methods are very difficult and require great skill and daring, but others are ridiculously simple. Practically every method depends on this secret: only the magician knows what he is going to do. Because your audience doesn't know what you are going to do until you've done it, they will never realize they were being forced at all. Here, for example, is an old force that is quite common and has worked well many times.

ANY BOY'S NAME

The magician writes something on a small slip of paper and drops it into an envelope. He seals the envelope and hands it to somebody for safe-keeping.

An open paper bag is placed on the table. The audience is a bit puzzled, and until now, the magician has said nothing. Now he speaks.

'Would you call out the names of any boys you know. First names only please.'

The audience begins to shout out names and the magician writes each name on a slip of paper and drops it into the paper bag. After collecting a number of names, he lays his pad and pencil aside and picks up the bag, shaking it to mix the slips. A member of the audience is invited to reach in and draw out one name. Let's say it is *Billy*.

The spectator holding the sealed envelope is invited to open it and on the slip of paper inside – written before anyone had called out a name or knew what was happening – is: *The name Billy will be chosen.*

HOW TO DO IT: Before reading the secret you should read the description of the trick again. This is the way your audience will see it. If it sounds impossible to you, you may feel certain that it will appear equally as impossible to your viewers. Remember, even after you read how it works, it will still seem as impossible to those people who are seeing your trick for the first time. Therefore please do not say 'Oh, that's silly, anyone will figure that out' . . . you haven't yet, have you?

Choose a very common name like Billy, John, Pete, Ken, or better still, some boy you know will be in the audience and write the name on a slip you seal in the envelope.

Ask people to call out names, but no matter what name they call out *you always write Billy* (or whatever name you wrote on the slip in the envelope).

You will have to be an actor and pretend to have trouble writing the harder names you receive, or ask 'How do you spell that?' or ask that certain names be repeated to be sure they are right . . . but you still write Billy!

It's easy to understand now why you were safe in writing your prediction of Billy on the slip in the envelope, and yet the spectator who chooses one slip out of the bag will feel certain that he is having a completely free selection. He is indeed having his free choice of any slip in the bag, and yet you are forcing him to choose Billy.

The best forces used by magicians are often this simple. Don't be misled by its simplicity, it allows you to do things just the way you would if you really were being fair. Your actions must appear perfectly natural but you must positively not give your helper any chance to make a mistake and select the object *he* wishes!

Suppose you wished to force the name *Herkermiah* or *Sigfried*, or some other name that you knew nobody in the audience would call out. You could still do it like the above, but it would be done a little differently. See if you can understand how this difference can help you before reading' HOW TO DO IT.

PICK A CRAZY NAME

Twenty slips of paper are passed out to the audience along with some pencils. They are asked to write the craziest name they can think of on their slip and fold it in half. When this has been done, the magician passes among the people and invites them to drop their slips into a paper bag he holds open.

Returning to the front of the room, he shakes the bag and mixes the slips. A spectator reaches in and selects one slip and reads aloud the name *Gertrude J. Manygrump.*

Sure enough, on a slip of paper the magician wrote before the trick began is found *Gertrude J. Manygrump!*

What's more, the slips in the bag can be dumped out and a few read just to prove they are really all different.

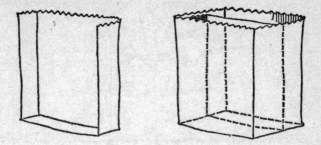

HOW TO DO IT: In case you haven't guessed yet, another name magician's use for this trick would be the *Paper Bag Force*. Magicians often make up their own names for their tricks.

Prepare a paper bag as shown in the illustration. You will need two paper bags of the same size, scissors and a little paste or glue.

Cut off the side of one of the bags, leaving half of the sides and bottom attached to it. Apply glue to the side and bottom flaps and drop it into the other bag so that it forms a divider down the centre. Allow this to dry, and you have produced a bag that looks like one bag from the outside but, inside, it is actually two bags.

Write the name you wish to force on twenty identical slips of paper from your pad. Fold each one in half and drop it on one side of the partition in the bag, leaving the other compartment empty. You are then prepared for the trick.

Simply pass out twenty identical slips of paper and a few pencils (they can share these) to your audience. Ask them to write a crazy name on each slip, fold them in half and drop them into the bag as you pass by.

As you collect the slips squeeze the partition to one side (see illustration) so their slips drop into the empty compartment. As you return to the front of the room and shake the bag, change hands and squeeze the partition over the

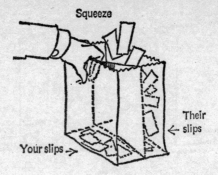

Squeeze

Their → slips

Your slips →

other way. This will open the compartment holding your names and seal off the side with the slips just written. The spectator will reach into the side with your names, and, naturally, be forced to choose what you want.

When your name is called out, every person in the room will immediately know it is not the name he wrote. He will simply assume that someone else wrote it so they will not question this odd name. You can then swap your hands on the bag again, seal off the compartment with your names, dump the audience's names out on to the table. Read off a few of these names ... besides showing people the names are all different, this can also be quite funny if the names are really crazy.

Think of all the words you can force this way: people, places, things, numbers, colours, animals, etc. The force is not a trick by itself, but it is an important tool a magician can use to help him to invent tricks of his own. I hope this chapter will help you develop your own ideas. After inventing one or two you will really begin to think like a magician and that is quite different from just reading how tricks are done.

Probably one of the most useful forces to a magician is making a person choose the playing card he (the magician) wishes from a deck of 52 different cards. There are hundreds of different ways magicians have devised for doing this one force. As you become more skilful you may wish to learn some of them; but for now, let us learn one simple card force that you will find useful for many tricks.

STOP ME ANYWHERE

The magician takes an ordinary deck of playing cards. He shows that they are all different and shuffles them. As the face of the deck is tipped towards the audience, the magician begins to pick cards off the top of the deck and drop them on the table.

'Stop me anywhere you like,' he says.

When the spectator stops him, he holds the deck out towards the spectator and asks that he pick off the next card on top.

All seems fair, yet this card will be the card the magician selected ahead of time for the spectator to choose. He not only knows what the card is, but he knew that the spectator was going to take it.

HOW TO DO IT: The cards are ordinary. They can even be a deck you borrow at someone's home. You can shuffle them as much as you like, but the card you wish to force should be *on the top of the deck*. As you shuffle you must keep that card on top of the deck. This is easy to do, but will require a little practice.

Hold the deck in one hand and draw cards out just as you would if you were giving them a regular overhand shuffle. Except, leave the top card in your hand and 'shuffle' the rest of the deck behind it. This will be an ordinary shuffle except the top card will still be on top when you're through. Try it with real cards and you will quickly learn how to do this naturally.

Next hold the deck in your hand so that your thumb

presses down on the top card (See illustration). Pull the top card back just a little with your thumb, and tip the cards up so the audience sees the faces and not the top of the deck. Begin pulling cards off the top with your other hand. You

can do this easily and because the top card is pulled back out of the way . . . it remains the top card!

If you were a card gambler, or a magician who specialised in card tricks, you would have a special name for what you are doing. You would be *dealing seconds*, that is, dealing out the second card each time, and leaving the first one in place.

As you deal seconds, ask to be stopped. When you are stopped you push the top card back into place with your thumb and hold the deck out towards the spectator.

He seems to have had a free choice, but he has actually been given the card you were saving for him!

Does this last force sound familiar to you? It is the first part of the orange trick you read about at the very beginning of this section. With this force you can easily make a person choose a duplicate of a card you have hidden inside one of the oranges, but there's more to the orange trick than that; you must also force him to choose the one orange out of four that contains the hidden card.

THE MAGICIAN'S CHOICE

This is not a trick so there is no description of it. The magician's choice is a way of making a person select one object from many by subtraction: By allowing a person to choose between half of those offered and taking away half with each choice he makes, the objects become fewer and fewer. Finally only one object remains. This object is the spectator's choice . . . or is it the magician's?

HOW TO DO IT: Again, notice how important it is for the spectator not to know beforehand what you are going to do. Do not tell him what, why, or how . . . just do it!

Any kind of object can be used, and any number of them. It is usually best and easiest, however, to choose a small even number. Two, four, or six objects work very well.

Suppose you had four fruits (an apple, a pear, a banana, and an orange) in front of you and you wanted to force the spectator to choose the orange. You might lay them out like this:

First, separate the fruits into two groups; the apple and pear in one, and the banana and orange in the other:

Ask the spectator to point to either group. Let's assume he points to the group on the left (apple/pear). You simply say 'OK let's lay them aside.' Push the apple/pear to the side and move the banana and the orange in front of him. Separate them a bit:

Again, ask him to point to either one. Whichever one he points to will give him the orange!

If he points to the banana, simply push that to one side saying, 'That leaves us with the orange.'

If he points towards the orange, pick it up and toss it to him saying, 'So you like the orange.'

Now, going back just a bit, suppose the first time he pointed to the orange/banana group instead of the apple/pear? You would have simply pushed the apple/pear group aside just as you did and say, 'The orange and banana are left, now would you please point to either of these.' In other words, you are going to do the same thing regardless of which group he points to. Because he doesn't know what you are doing, he certainly will not know whether you are doing it right or wrong!

Do not be afraid to try the magician's choice. It sounds as though your audience will quickly catch on to what you are doing, but it won't. Also, this trick should never be used all by itself; the magician's choice is always just a small part of a much larger and more exciting effect.

The card in the orange trick is a perfect example of a more wonderful trick. It uses two forces: a card and one orange. Because it uses these, it is a good one to learn right now.

The *Card In The Orange* trick is described at the start of this section. The trick can be divided into five parts you must learn:

1 Forcing the correct card
2 Making the card vanish from the envelope
3 Putting a duplicate card in one orange
4 Forcing a person to select this orange
5 Making the torn corners match

Let's learn how to accomplish each of these one by one. Remember that no single one of them is a trick in itself. I will leave it for you to work them smoothly together to accomplish the trick in the way you read about earlier.

1 *Forcing the card.* You will need two cards that are the same. (Every magician-to-be should purchase two match-

ing decks of cards; he will often find them useful.) One card is set aside for steps three and five, the other is put on top of the deck. This card will be forced as described earlier.

2 *Making the card vanish from the envelope.* The easiest way to do this is by simply never putting it in the envelope in the first place. Tear the card into six pieces and slip them *behind* the envelope, holding them in place with your thumb. From the front it will appear that you have put them inside. Seal the envelope and push it into your pocket. Drop the pieces into your pocket, but leave some of the envelope poking out. (Be sure the audience can't see through your shirt pocket.) Later, when you remove the envelope you simply leave the pieces behind.

3 *Putting the duplicate card in one orange.* Tear one corner off the duplicate card and set it aside for step five. Roll the card, long way, around a pencil to form it into a tube. Remove the pencil and roll the card into a still thinner tube.

Take an orange, the larger the better, and pick off the small pip (the end of the stem) and *keep it.* Poke a pencil into the soft part of the orange that you will find under the pip and push the card down into this hole. Using the pencil, shove the card completely inside the orange. This, you will discover, is very simple.

Dip the end of the pip you save into some glue and stick it back on the end of the orange to hide the hole containing the card. Later, no matter how closely the orange is examined, nobody will discover how the card got inside.

4 *Forcing a person to select this orange.* Use the *Magician's Choice* described earlier. This time you will be using all the same objects, oranges, but by dividing them into groups of two you can proceed in exactly the same way.

Because you will be forcing one orange from several oranges you must secretly mark the one with the card inside so you will know which one to force. You might make a small pencil mark on it or pull the pips off all the unprepared oranges. This will never be noticed, but will show you instantly which one is to be forced. Whatever way you choose to mark it ... always remember to do something which will let you recognize the orange containing the card before you start the trick. Imagine how embarrassing it would be if you couldn't!

5 *Making the torn corners match.* To do the trick it is not necessary to make the torn corners match ... the card you find in the orange could be whole. However, the torn corner is a little touch you can include just to make the trick even more baffling and more fun.

You have torn off a corner of the card in the orange in step number three. Place this torn corner *inside* the envelope *before* doing step number two.

As you perform the trick after forcing the cards, tearing it up, and placing the pieces 'in' the envelope, reach inside and remove this special corner piece. Say, 'perhaps you might like to keep one piece as a souvenir', and hand it to the spectator for safe keeping. Later, this will naturally match the corner of the card discovered in the orange ... because that's where it came from!

Many people who just *think* they want to become magicians will not bother to spend time learning how to force objects or words. They will quickly realize that these are not tricks by themselves, and they will jump ahead to search for more obvious secrets. The force, however, is a very important part of a real magician's education ... it is another 'tool of his trade'. Knowing how to use *all* his tools makes a better carpenter than one who only knows how to use a hammer ... the tools of magic and magicians are very much like that.

CHAPTER 5

GIMMICKS – INVISIBLE ASSISTANTS

Probably no single word in the very special vocabulary that magicians use is better known than *gimmick*. The word is actually just a slang expression which means the 'hidden thing'. For example, if someone offered to give you a pound note for a penny, you might say, 'What's the catch?' or, 'There must be a gimmick in that offer.' This suggests what the word gimmick means to a magician.

If you look the word up in a dictionary you might find something like: *Any small device used secretly by a magician in performing a trick*. The real 'magic word' in this definition is *secretly*. A gimmick may be something quite familiar to the audience, or something very specially made to do a particular job. A gimmick may be simply something special you do to an object that the audience can see, but something which must always be secret. It must be important in making the trick work, but it must be completely unknown to the audience. Certainly a gimmick is something you should know about! Just to get started, you can do a most amazing card trick with the aid of a very simple gimmick.

THIS CARD IS YOUR CARD

The magician fans a deck of cards out towards a spectator and invites him to choose one, look at it, remember it, and replace it in the deck anywhere he chooses.

When this has been done, the deck is given a thorough shuffle. The magician even hands the deck to the spectator and invites him to give the cards one final mixing.

He takes the deck back, glances through the cards quickly and removes one card face down.

'What card did you select?' he asks.

The spectator names his card.

'Ah,' says the magician, 'then I believe this card is your card.'

He turns the card he is holding over and it is the same one the spectator named.

HOW TO DO IT: The *Pick A Card* trick is one of the oldest, and best-known, magic tricks. Because it is so well associated with magicians, every young magician should learn a way of doing it for that special time he is asked to perform at a party or a friend's home. There are probably a thousand different ways magicians have invented for letting a spectator choose a card.

Some methods require special cards, remembering certain cards in the deck, having the selected card returned in a special place, or special shuffles which don't really mix the cards. If, however, you were a real magician, you would need none of these things ... you would let the person choose any card, return it anywhere, shuffle the deck himself, and you would still be able to find his card. This is exactly what you appear to do in this trick, but, unfortunately, you're not a real magician so you do require the help of your invisible assistant ... a gimmick. Have you guessed what it might be?

You may use your own deck of cards for this trick, or to make it appear fairer you can use your friend's cards. Whichever you use, however, you will also require a pencil and a few moments alone to prepare the cards.

Hold the deck tightly together with the edges of all the cards lined up. Draw a single, fairly light, pencil line down the middle of one side. That single pencil line is your gimmick!

Once you have drawn the line, be certain to keep the cards facing the same way so the pencil dot (because that's what it looks like now on a single card) always faces towards the same side. You can easily shuffle the deck and mix the cards thoroughly, still keeping the dots on the same side.

47

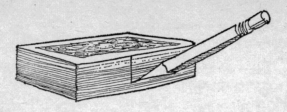

Allow your helper to select a card, look at it and place it back in the deck ... but ... while he is looking at it you must secretly *turn the deck halfway around*. When he pushes his card back in, the pencil dot on it will be on the other side from those on all the other cards. Now carefully shuffle the cards. You can mix the cards as much as you like, but do not twist them or you will mix up the pencil dots. You can even, quite safely, hand them to your assistant. He will not mix up the pencil marks.

When you finally receive the deck, simply glance at the edge as you fan them out. Look for the single pencil-marked card in the plain side of the deck. That will be his card and you can easily slip your fingernail under it to help separate it from the deck. Be sure to pretend to be looking through the deck, at the faces of the cards, this way your assistant never suspects what you are really doing.

Once your trick is done you can safely repeat it for someone else if you wish. When you are ready to put the cards away, however, remember to mix them thoroughly. Be sure to turn some one way and some the other. This way nobody will later notice your pencil line running down the side. The simple pencil line is your gimmick, and it must remain a secret to your audience.

A gimmick can be used to make a very ordinary piece of apparatus do something that the apparatus could never do if it was as plain as it appears to be. Many clever young magicians enjoy making their own pieces of equipment, and learning how to gimmick them adds to the fun. Here's an easy one you can start with.

CLIPPING CLIPS

An ordinary looking soup tin is sitting on the table, along with a saucer containing a dozen paper clips. Picking up two of the clips, the magician hooks them together to make a paper clip chain.

'I'm sure you have all clipped paper clips together like this, and added still more to make a long chain. There is no magic to this, but I would like to show you how a magician might do it by magic.'

He picks up the clips from the saucer and drops them, one at a time, into the tin. He counts them as they fall.

'One, two, three, four, five, six, seven, eight, nine, ten and the two I've already linked make twelve. Now watch.'

He picks the tin up and dumps the clips into his hand.

'Clips . . . CLIP.'

As he says the magic word he tosses the clips into the air and they fall back into his waiting hand all clipped together in a long continuous chain.

HOW TO DO IT: You will require twenty-four paper clips, the bigger the better. Twelve of these should be linked together to form a long chain. The other twelve are left separate and will remain in the saucer in case anyone should want to see them. You will also need a special gimmicked tin:

Open a tin with your mother's tin opener. Any tin will work well. Do not open the top all the way around, but leave the cover attached to the tin with a little piece of metal. Fold the cover pack with a pair of pliers (do not use your fingers to bend the cover, the metal is very sharp) and then pour out the contents of the tin. Wash the tin out thoroughly.

Using the pliers, fold the top of the tin down, then back

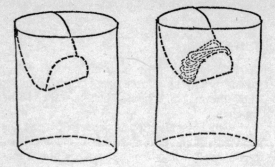

inside the tin to make a little 'V' shaped shelf inside. The illustrations will help you do this properly.

Fold the *linked* string of clips back and forth to make a compact bundle and drop it on to the shelf inside the tin. (Again, refer to the illustration.) Place the tin, with the clips hidden inside, on the table. Place the saucer holding the twelve unlinked clips beside it and you're ready to try out this trick.

Link two of the clips in the saucer together to show the audience how it's actually done. Then pick the other clips off the saucer and drop them one at a time, as you count, *into* the tin. Be sure they go beside the shelf right to the bottom.

After the clips are in the tin (including the two linked

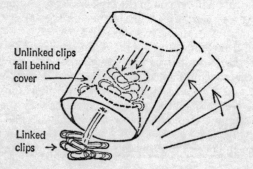

Unlinked clips
fall behind
cover →

Linked
clips →

ones) tip the tin over to dump them out on to your palm. This is done in a special way. Be sure to tip the tin so that the edge with the cover still attached is down towards your hand. You will find that the trick then works itself; the unlinked clips will remain trapped in the can, and the bundle of linked clips fall out into your hand. When the linked clips are shown in a bunch nobody will be able to tell that they are already joined. And because the tin was turned upside down as you dumped them out it appears that it must now be empty. You can place the tin on the table *upside down* (otherwise the loose clips left inside will make a noise) and push it to one side. Toss the clips from your hand into the air and allow them to spread out as they go. It will appear that they became linked while they were in the air.

One favourite kind of magic trick is called *Sucker Trick*. A sucker is a slang expression for a person who is easily fooled and confused. A sucker trick allows the audience to think they are more clever than the magician, and they're sure they have figured out his trick. But in the end they are 'suckers' because he succeeds in fooling them all. It's easy to fool an audience if you use something they don't know about. That makes you just one step smarter than they are, and that, you will see, is how sucker tricks work!

GUESS AGAIN!

The magician suggests that he is going to present a short test to discover how carefully the audience is watching what he is doing. He shows a box, quite empty – but says nothing about its being so as the audience can see it without being told. He sets it open-end-up on the table. Picking up three squares of cardboard he names each colour as he drops them into the box.

'First I will drop a yellow card into the box. Please watch carefully and try to remember the colours. Next a green card. And finally a red one.

'Now, watch carefully.' He reaches into the box and removes a red card. 'What colour is this card?'

He takes out the yellow card and again asks the audience to name its colour.

'Now, you haven't had any trouble as long as you have been able to see the cards. Let's make the test a bit harder. What colour card is left in the box?'

The audience shouts back Green!

Reaching into the box, the magician removes a RED card. 'See I knew you were not watching closely enough!'

The audience is surprised at seeing the red card, but only for a moment. They quickly decide that the green card is simply on the other side of the red one.

'Turn it around,' the audience shouts.

The magician turns the card around, but by twisting it upside down, he still keeps the red side forward.

'No, No!' shouts the audience, 'the other way!'

The magician obliges by twisting the card around the other way, as they asked. That is, he twists it, still red side forward, back in the other direction.

The audience screams louder. They are certain that they know how the trick is done. 'Let's see the back side,' they shout.

'Oh,' says the magician, 'you mean this side?' He flips the card over.

Written across the back of the card are the words FOOLED YOU. At the same time he lifts the box and tips it towards the audience to show that there are no cards left inside.

'See,' he explains, 'I knew that you were not watching me closely enough. You'll never figure out how any of my tricks work if you don't watch much more carefully.'

HOW TO DO IT: For this trick you must gimmick two of the three cards, but this is easily done. You will make the cards from some stiff red, green, and yellow paper. You can make them any size you wish, depending on the size of the audience you will show them to. Glue, scissors, and a cardboard box large enough to hold the cards are the other necessary items.

First you should prepare the cards. The audience guesses that the cards are not quite as they appear, but they are not prepared in the way they figure out.

You must cut squares from the paper in the size you choose to make the finished cards. Cut one square of yellow, one square of green, and two squares of red.

Paste one of the red squares on to the green square to produce a card that is red on one side and green on the other. Trim the edges with your scissors so none of the colour from the back shows from the front.

On the plain square of red paper print the words FOOLED YOU in big black letters. The other side is left plain blank red.

To prepare for the trick, place the box on your table with the three cards beside it. The cards should be stacked this way:

1 Lay the red card on the table with the side saying FOOLED YOU facing down.
2 On top of this place the green/red card with the red side down.
3 On top of this place the plain yellow card.

Show the box empty and replace it flat on the table to begin the actual trick. Pick up the yellow card and tip it towards the audience, asking them to name its colour. Drop it into the box.

Pick up the next card and turn it so the top (green) side faces the audience and ask what colour it is. Drop it into the box.

Pick up the last card with the plain red side showing. Ask its colour and drop it into the box.

Now talk for a moment about observing and then reach into the box and take out the plain yellow card. When the audience names its colour lay it aside.

53

Next remove the double card, but *turn it over before you remove it so that the red side shows* and ask the audience to name its colour. They will see the colour and say red! This then leaves you with only the special red card remaining in the box. Now set the double card aside.

Ask what colour is left in the box. The audience will answer 'green' because that is the one colour they haven't been shown. Remove the final card, plain red side forward, and wait. People will quickly tell you to 'turn it around'. After having your fun, convincing the audience that you do indeed have something to hide on the back side, flip it over to show the FOOLED YOU written on the back.

After a moment your audience may suggest that the missing green card is still inside the box. Let them suggest this but pretend not to hear them. When they really are fully convinced this must be the explanation, tip the box over and show it empty. This is your final proof that you are truly the magician and that they are actually nothing but a lot of 'suckers'.

Probably the very best kind of magic is that which uses only common everyday items which everyone recognizes. These are ofter easily gimmicked by the magician but are seldom suspected by the audience. If, for example, paper cups and water are used in a trick, very few people would ever expect the gimmick to be cups without bottoms! This, however, is the gimmick of the next trick which is one of the most surprising ones described in this entire book. You will find it is well worth making, practising, and presenting.

DEHYDRATED WATER

The magician has four paper cups lined up on the table. He proceeds to demonstrate that each one is quite empty.

Holding up his finger and thumb squeezed together, he explains that he has invented this 'pill' of dehydrated water. 'All we need is this pill and a little air.'

He drops the imaginary pills into two of the cups. Lifting the other two cups, he scoops them through the air to 'catch a little air' and turns them upside down over each of the two cups on the table.

He waits a moment for the 'air to mix well with the dehydrated water,' he removes the top cups and pours real water into them from the two bottom cups.

HOW TO DO IT: Actually you must use six cups in this trick but the audience will see only four. Two will always be hidden inside two of the others, but from a short distance this will not be noticed.

To begin, obtain six *heavy* paper cups. The paper should be thick enough so nothing inside can be seen through from the outside. All the cups should be the same size, and should look identical.

With a pair of scissors cut out the bottoms of two of the cups. You don't have to remove the entire bottom, just a large hole will do nicely.

Arrange the cups on the table as shown. Cups three and four should be about *half-filled* with water.

Note: After setting up the trick as shown in the illustrations, if the double rims on the two cups at positions three and four are too obvious, you might cut the rims off the cups which will hold the water.

If your audience is a short distance away, however, they will not see the double rims and you will find the rim is handy for lifting the cups secretly. Try it both ways.

1
(Plain cup)

2
(Bottomless cup)

3
(Plain cup of water inside bottomless cup)

4
(Two plain cups, inner one with water)

If you can actually have the cups in front of you as you read these directions, you will find the trick very simple to understand. If not, the illustrations will help make the moves clearer.

First you must show all cups 'empty'. Do this quickly and do not mention water or what the trick is all about.

Like most tricks, this one should end in a real surprise.

To show the cups empty you must do the following moves: First, simply pick up the unprepared cup (number one) and show it empty. Pick it up, turn it over, allow the audience to see inside, and say, 'These four cups are all identical. This one fits perfectly into this one,' and *drop cup number one into cup number two.*

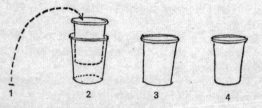

Remove cup number one and set it back in its original place on the table. Pick up number two cup and tip it *sideways* to the audience to prove that it is also empty. Be sure to hold it sideways so nobody can see inside and notice that it actually has no bottom. Naturally, everyone will assume it is just like the first cup.

Now say, 'And this cup just fits inside this one,' and drop it into cup(s) number three.

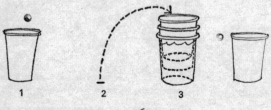

As before, remove the cup and replace it on the table, but this time *catch the inner cup from number three and lift it right out with cup number two*. This is easy to do, and when you set cup number two back on the table it will actually be inside the cup filled with water that was previously inside cup number three. This leaves only a bottomless cup, without water, in spot number three.

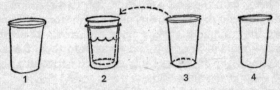

Now pick up cup number three, tip it sideways and show that it is empty (again, keeping it sideways because it is bottomless). Continue by saying, 'And this cup fits nicely into the last.' Drop the bottomless cup number three into cup number four.

Remove cup number three, *and the inner cup from number four as a single cup* and set them down in position number three.

If you have followed these moves carefully, either with real cups or your imagination, you will understand now why the audience is quite convinced that you have shown that every cup is empty. Yet, you have succeeded in secretly shifting two half-full cups of water right under their noses.

To finish the trick you simply pretend to drop a 'dehydrated water pill' into the cups numbered two and three. Pick up cups one and four and pretend to scoop up some air with them. Turn them upside down over two and three and allow a moment or two for the 'pills' and air to mix.

Once the 'mixing' has taken place, remove the upper cups one at a time and pour the real water into them from the lower cups. Pour the water back and forth between the cups just to show everyone that the water is real.

As with all tricks, this one will require a little practice. You will find that you must lower the bottomless cups into the water-filled ones slowly. To disguise this fact you should practice lowering *all* of them slowly.

You must also practice *lifting* the cups. You must learn to pick up the water-filled ones as though they were empty.

You must simply learn to treat all the cups the same regardless of whether they are empty or filled. This is the real 'magic' you must master to make this one of the most amazing tricks you can present.

Like the 'holes' in the bottom of the cups in the above trick, gimmicks are often the little differences that make an audience sit up and pay attention. Frequently, to explain how his tricks work, a magician will blame it all on his 'invisible helper'. To his audience the idea of an invisible helper suggests a ghost or spook and they generally laugh at this ridiculous suggestion. Often, however, this explanation is very truthful from the magician's side because his definition of an invisible assistant is probably a *gimmick* . . . something quite invisible to the audience, but very necessary to the magician. Surely a gimmick is an important tool in the magician's trade.

CHAPTER 6

APPEARANCES – MAKING SOMETHING FROM NOTHING

Producing something from nothing must surely be the most wondrous trick that any magician can perform. It certainly is one of the most common magic tricks.

From his empty hands, hat, or box, the magician is able to draw out an amazing variety of solid objects. It appears that he has created these objects from thin air. Getting something from nothing is both a scientific impossibility and a dream that many of us have. Because of these two facts, the magical appearance is a very important trick in every magic show.

Very simply, the appearance or production follows a very logical series of steps which require only one subtraction to make it mysterious. Suppose, for example, you wanted to take a glass of water out of an empty hat; here's how you would do it:

1 Show a hat empty.
2 Put a glass of water into the hat.
3 Take the glass of water out of the hat.

But that's not magic, that's the way ordinary people do it! The subtraction you must do, is to eliminate step number two.

Now, of course you can't eliminate step number two. You must put the glass of water into the hat. So this step is not only necessary, but it is also impossible to avoid. Your job, however, is to do step number two so that no one knows you have done it. This sounds difficult and it certainly requires some nerve on your part, but it is actually quite simple. In fact, causing a glass of water to appear in a hat will be a good way to begin.

WATER SURPRISE

The magician shows a hat quite empty, and a small red rubber ball. He places the ball into the hat.

The hat is turned over and the ball is gone. The magician takes it out of his coat pocket. He repeats this several times.

Finally he places the ball in his pocket and causes it to appear back in the hat. Unfortunately, the magician is not very clever and the audience sees him hiding the ball in his hand. People quickly begin to shout, 'I know how you're doing it.'

'Do you really know?' asks the magician. 'Were you really watching very closely?'

The audience shouts, 'Yes!' and the people feel certain that they have caught him.

'Well then,' asks the magician, 'Perhaps you could explain where this glass of water came from?'

He reaches into the hat and removes a small glass full of water which he pours into a pitcher on the table!

HOW TO DO IT: This is a most unusual trick because to do it you must practice being very clumsy as well as being very clever. Your clumsiness helps you in tricking the audience.

You will require four things for this trick. You will need an old felt hat. You can borrow one from your dad, or use a small cardboard box if he won't loan you one. You will need a small glass of water. Buy a 'shot' glass if your mother doesn't have one. And you will need two duplicate *rubber* balls. Experiment a bit to be sure the glass and the balls 'fit' properly. The ball should be just a bit larger than the mouth of the glass. If you push the ball into the glass filled with water, the suction should hold it in place. The glass and the ball must be small enough to hide in your hand.

To prepare for the trick, push one ball hard into the glass

of water and drop it, glass and all, into your pocket. The ball will be held tightly against the glass so the water will not spill. Drop the other ball into the same pocket.

Practice this trick in front of a mirror.

First, show the hat empty. Reach into your pocket and remove the separate ball. Pretend to drop it into the hat but really hide it in your hand and take it right out again. Say, 'I will put this ball into the hat and,' reach back into your pocket with the hand hiding the ball, 'it jumps right back into my pocket.' Remove the ball from your pocket and show it. Repeat this several times. Be sure to *be a little clumsy* when you do this (if your hands are small and the audience sees the ball, that is perfect) so the audience quickly begins to catch on to what you are doing. It is important, in fact, that they realize that you are not really putting the ball into the hat.

Once people realize what you are doing they will begin to tell you about it. When this happens you are ready for your secret move.

Say, 'Let me show you that this ball can also go the other way around,' and place the separate ball into your pocket. 'I'll put the ball in my pocket and . . .,' pick up the ball with the glass on it and move it to the hat. (Don't worry if your audience sees you do this. Again your clumsiness is part of the trick.) '. . . it jumps right back into the hat.'

Hold the glass in the hat and remove the ball with your other hand. You can be sure that the audience will tell you they 'saw you put the ball back in the hat.' Let them yell for a while, because you are now ready to fool them.

Slowly place the ball back into your pocket saying, 'Do you really know how I did this trick?' They will tell you they do. 'Then,' you explain as you reach slowly into the hat, 'could you tell me where this glass of water came from?' Reach slowly into the hat and remove the glass of water. Pour the water into a pitcher.

You can be certain that the glass of water will surprise

your audience, and nobody will be able to tell you where it came from. At first you presented a mystery to your audience which they thought they could explain, but then you gave them a completely different one. So rather than being a clumsy magician, you have suddenly turned the tables and succeeded in mystifying everyone. Try it, and see if it doesn't leave your audience dumbfounded.

A sudden appearance of something from nothing is certainly exciting. For this reason many magicians find that an appearance is one of the best ways to start a magic show. It is a promise, to your audience, of the wonders they will be seeing. Perhaps you too would like to begin your show with a quick, snappy, unexplainable production. Try this one:

THE SILK SURPRISE

The magician walks forward with a sheet of paper which he shows on both sides. He crumples it into a ball, breaks through the paper and begins to pull out a corner of a colourful silk handkerchief. He continues pulling until a very large silk handkerchief has been produced from the empty sheet of paper.

HOW TO DO IT: One of the prettiest 'props' used by magicians is the silk handkerchief. Every magician-to-be should possess at least one or two. For this trick you will require one very colourful silk handkerchief, about 24 inches square. You can purchase one at any department store, or your mother or sister may have one you can borrow.

One reason magicians use silk handkerchiefs, which they simply call *silks*, is that they can be folded and squeezed into very small bundles which are easily hidden, and yet they open up into surprisingly large squares when unfolded. You will use this principle in the next trick.

Fold your silk into a small square and roll the square up into a small ball. With a little experimenting you will be

able to fold it into a very small bundle. Wrap a black thread around this bundle and tie it in place. Leave about ten inches of thread on the end.

Many people believe that black thread helps the magician with many of his tricks, but acually very few tricks use it.

This, however, is one trick which uses thread. You could use blue, green or yellow though, and it would work just as well.

You will also need a sheet of paper about 20 inches square. Newspapers will work very well. Fasten the free end of your thread to the centre of one of the edges of the paper with sticky tape. Place the bundled silk in your outer breast pocket, and you're ready to go. The illustration will help to make this clear.

This is an 'opening trick' because you must be holding the paper when you start. You cannot pick it up, or put it down, until you are finished. You must walk out holding the paper in front of your coat with the edge of the thread taped to it at the top.

Show the front of the paper to your audience. Tip the paper up from the bottom so they can see the back side. Tip the paper back to its original position and move your hands

forward. This action will pull the silk bundle out of your pocket and it will swing into place behind the paper.

To finish the trick, bring your hands together and crumple the paper into a ball around the silk bundle. Break through the paper and draw out a corner of the kerchief. You will find it is easy to draw it free of its thread-binding and out of the paper. Once it is free, toss the paper ball aside, show the silk and . . . now that you have proven that you are indeed a magician . . . on with the show!

Naturally you should not do one appearance trick after another because they would soon bore the audience. The appearance is just a tool of the magician's trade and should be a part, not a whole of the magic show. Many magicians become so interested in production tricks that they do one right after another. This is as foolish as a carpenter who became so interested in his hammer that he never bothered to find out about a saw. Imagine how funny his house would look. Here is another appearance. It appears quite different from the above, but it is still a something-from-nothing trick so please don't do it right after the *Silk Surprise*.

TIED BUT TRUE

A piece of clothesline rope is shown. It is tied to the magician's wrists leaving a short length of rope between his hands.

'Watch carefully and you will be surprised,' says the magician.

He turns around so that his back hides his hands from the audience for just a moment. When he turns around again he is still tied as before, but a large handkerchief is seen hanging from the centre of the rope.

'Could someone explain to me where this handkerchief came from?' he asks apparently quite puzzled.

To remove the handkerchief, either the rope or the handkerchief must be untied. As this is done, the audience ponders the sudden appearance of the handkerchief in the centre of the rope in that fraction of a second while the magician's back was turned and his hands were securely tied.

HOW TO DO IT: An ordinary pocket handkerchief may be used for this sudden appearance, but a colourful one will

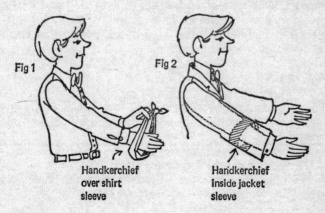

Fig 1 — Handkerchief over shirt sleeve

Fig 2 — Handkerchief inside jacket sleeve

make this trick even more beautiful. Tie two diagonal corners of the handkerchief together and slip your hand through the hole in the centre. Slide the handkerchief up your arm and inside your jacket sleeve. (See illustration.) The audience should not be aware of this handkerchief up your sleeve.

Give a helper a piece of clothesline rope about three feet long and instruct him to tie one end to one of your wrists. Hold the other wrist a short distance away from the tied one and ask him to tie the other end of the rope to it. This will leave a short length of rope between your two wrists. Naturally your audience will not know what you're going to do, but many will suspect that you are going to escape from the ties; this is good because the appearance of the handkerchief will surprise them all the more.

When you turn your back, simply reach up your sleeve and pull the handkerchief down on to the centre of the rope. Immediately turn around and ask, 'Where did this handkerchief come from?'

One other appearance trick you might like to master is one that depends on 'sleight-of-hand'. This is using your hands to hide something and causing the audience to believe that it appears. This type of trick requires both skill and nerve, properly done, however, it is almost inexplicable. Magicians sometimes call this kind of trick where an extra object appears, a *multiplication*.

A BALL FROM THE AIR

The magician removes three small paper balls from his pocket and places them in his left palm. He holds out his opened hand.

'How many balls do you see?'

'Three,' answers the spectator.

The magician spills the balls into his right hand, and asks,

'Do you still see three balls?'

'Yes.'

He asks the spectator to hold out his hand, and pours the balls into the spectator's hand. He folds the assistant's hand into a fist hiding the balls inside.

'How many balls are you holding?'

'Three.'

'Are you sure?'

'Yes.'

'Well here, let me add another one,' says the magician as he appears to roll still another, completely imaginary ball, and tosses it towards the assistant's hand. 'Open your hand.'

The assistant opens his hand and discovers four paper balls inside.

HOW TO DO IT: You must use four paper balls for this trick. You should roll them out of tiny sheets of paper about three inches square. Be sure that each ball looks like the others. Place the four balls in your right coat pocket.

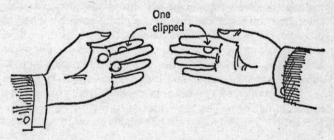

As you begin the trick, reach into your pocket with your right hand and remove *all* four balls. However, and this is the secret, clip one of them between your fingers. (See illustration.) Turn your hand over on the table and allow three of them to fall on to the tabletop. The extra ball remains clipped between your fingers.

Ask how many balls your helper sees. Pick up the three balls with your *left* hand and let them roll on to your palm. As you ask how many balls your helper sees, clip one of them between your fingers. Turn your left hand over on to your right hand and let the *two* free balls on to your right palm. These two balls, together with the extra one already clipped between your right fingers, will make three balls showing in your right palm. Ask how many your helper sees there.

Holding the extra ball clipped in your right palm, turn the right hand over on top of your left. Two balls will spill into your left hand, but thanks to the extra ball clipped there, you helper will see three in your left palm.

When he is convinced that you have only three balls which you are simply passing from hand to hand, ask him to open one of his hands. Dump the *three* balls (all of them) from your left hand into your right. Pour *all* of the balls, including the extra one from your right hand, into his open hand. Use your left hand to help him close his fingers into a fist around the balls.

Properly done, he will be convinced that he holds only three balls in his closed fist . . . watch his surprise when he finally opens it and discovers four!

An appearance is as important to a magic show as an engine is to an automobile. People expect magicians to make something from nothing and they are seldom disappointed. See how many you can observe the next time you watch a magician perform. The appearance is probably the most important trick that a magician has 'up his sleeve.'

CHAPTER 7

VANISHES – NOW YOU SEE IT . . NOW YOU DON'T

His girl assistant stands on the top of a small table and the magician tosses a silk cloth over her. Her form is fully visible under the drape. There is a roll of drums, a sudden puff of green smoke and the cloth falls limp on the table . . . the girl seems to have dissolved!

Later the magician entertains a young boy who has come back-stage to meet him. He shows the boy a playing card and a coin. His hands are perfectly empty as he places the coin on top of the card and turns the two upside down and lays them on the table. When the boy picks up the card, the coin is gone!

To the magician these tricks are just the same. One perhaps is harder to do and requires more apparatus, but the same thing happens to the girl as happens to the coin . . . the magician makes them vanish! The vanish, big or small, fast or slow, easy or hard, is a common trick you will see in any magic show. Certainly anyone who wants to call himself a magician should be able to make things disappear. Even if it really is impossible to do, you can learn how to appear to make things vanish.

Like an *appearance* trick, a vanish follows three logical steps:

(Let's use the coin under the card vanish as an example.)

1 Put the coin under the card.
2 Take the coin out from under the card.
3 Lift the card to show the coin is gone.

This is, naturally, the way most people would do this. Only if you could eliminate step number two would you really be a magician. The magican's job however, is just that

... you must make people feel that you have eliminated step number two. Actually you have just changed it: *sneak* the coin out from under the card. Then, with a little acting on your part you are ready to convince your audience that the coin vanished. How to do that is the purpose of this section.

ONE CARD PLUS ONE COIN EQUALS ONE CARD

The magician lays a playing card on the fingers of his opened hand. He places a coin on top of the card and holds it against the card with his thumb. Turning his hand over he lays the card down on the table with the coin underneath.

A spectator is invited to pick up the card. He discovers that is all there is on the table ... one card. The coin is gone.

HOW TO DO IT: The illustration will best show you how to hold the card and the coin. Your thumb should be on top of the card to hold the coin against it. Your fingers should be extended straight under the card.

Turn the card over and place it down on the table. Let the coin strike the tabletop so your audience hears it thump, but do not let go of it with your thumb.

As you slip your hand and thumb away to leave the card on the table, continue to hold the coin with your thumb. Pull it away drawing the coin with it. The coin will come away from the card and be hidden by your fingers. Remove your hand with the coin hidden inside and drop it into your pockets as you invite someone to pick up the card.

This is a sleight-of-hand trick. It will require a lot of skill, and a great deal of practice. Please try it many times by yourself before you try it on a friend.

When you appear to make an object vanish and you tell your audience that it has disappeared, you have actually hidden it from view. For this reason, a word you might like to add to your magic vocabulary is *steal*. This is what a magician does when he removes an object in some manner not seen by the audience. So, to make an object vanish, you must make a steal. To make an object appear you must also, surprisingly, make a steal. In other words, you must steal an object (unknown to the audience) and place it somewhere where it will appear later. This is another time when the magician must play the part of an actor – and play it very well.

YOU KNOW IT'S THERE BUT IT'S NOT

'Let me show you how to make a coin vanish,' says the magician as he removes a handkerchief and a coin from his pocket.

He spreads the handkerchief out over his palm and lays the coin in the centre. Holding the coin with his fingers, he flips the handkerchief over so its corners hang down.

'Now, on the count of three I will make this coin vanish before your eyes. Are you ready? Don't blink or you will miss it. One . . . two . . .'

The magician pauses, as though someone in the audience suspects that the coin has already been stolen away.

'Wait! Perhaps you do not believe that the coin is really

71

under the handkerchief? Well before I make it vanish it is certainly important that you all know that it is truly there. I would like each one of you to reach under the cloth and feel the coin.'

He walks into the audience and invites each person to reach under and feel the coin. He asks each person if they feel it, and each person answers 'Yes.' Walking back to the front of the room, he says:

'Do you all agree that the coin is indeed under the handkerchief? Yes. Well watch carefully. One . . . two . . . three!'

With a flip, the magician tosses the handkerchief towards the spectators and the coin is gone. He holds his hands high so nobody can suspect he is hiding it. The coin is truly gone.

HOW TO DO IT: When you first read how this trick is accomplished you will probably say, 'That's an unfair trick,' and so it is. Remember that you can use any method as long as it succeeds in fooling your audience.

You may be sure that everyone will think you are a fine magician because, no matter how carefully they watch you, nobody will ever see you steal the coin away. They won't see you because you never do it. In fact, you don't even do this trick at all. A friend of yours does.

You will need a friend who is going to be sitting in the audience watching the show, or perhaps he might be standing with a group of other friends who want to see a trick. He must be a friend who is willing to practice ahead of time with you. He should be someone the audience will not suspect, and yet, someone you know can keep a secret. Magicians call this kind of friend a *stooge*, even though this name does not sound very complimentary. To a magician, however, a stooge is simply a friend who appears to be just another spectator. Actually he's a very trusted helper. Often, as in this trick, your stooge must have as much nerve as a magician.

Proceed with the trick just as described above. Show the

coin and hide it under the handkerchief. Allow each person (if the group is small enough, or just a few if it is larger) to reach under and feel the coin. Be sure your stooge is the *last* person to feel it. When he does he simply *takes the coin*. He hides it in his hand and later, when you return to the front of the room, he drops it unnoticed into his pocket.

You return with the handkerchief quite empty, but you must still do a bit of acting and pretend that it is still there. Remind the audience that they have all felt the coin. Then count to three and toss the handkerchief towards them. Be sure to show that your hands are empty and allow members of the audience to pick up the handkerchief and examine it. This is one trick where you should do everything you can to convince the audience that you did not sneak out the coin and are not hiding it any place.

You can use this same method to vanish any small object that your friend's hand can hold: a small ball, an egg, or a sweet. It is even possible to make a pencil vanish this way by having your friend drop it down his sleeve.

Remember that the audience will not be watching carefully while people reach under the handkerchief and feel the coin. In fact they will probably become bored with watching you ask all your friends to do the same. This feeling under the handkerchief appears very fair. They will not think the trick is really underway until you return to the front of the room.

We should remember another important rule a good magician will obey: remember your audience! You should always do tricks that are suited for the audience to whom you are showing them. Remember that girls and ladies like pretty tricks, animals, and things they know about. Older boys like tricks that look dangerous, impossible or funny. Small children like animals, funny tricks and things they recognize. With small children try to remember that you should never use cards or other things which they may not understand or know.

73

A good magician always chooses different tricks for different audiences. If you use tricks your audience enjoys, you will succeed in becoming a popular magician. Remember your audience!

Some of the very best magic tricks are those that use objects which everyone recognizes and you use them to do something that everyone understands. These are magical surprises, and everyone enjoys a surprise. Here is an example of a familiar object, a piece of rope, behaving in a most peculiar way.

A VANISH THAT'S KNOT

'A magician's job is to try to fool you,' says the magician as he picks up a box that contains a deck of cards.

'Let me warn you that I will always be trying to do just that . . . so watch carefully or you will be fooled.'

He opens up the card box but, instead of a deck of cards he pulls out a length of rope!

'See! You thought I was going to do a card trick. I've fooled you once already! Now I'm going to try to fool you again.'

He ties a single knot in the centre of the rope.

'I am going to make this knot vanish before your eyes. Would you like to see it vanish visibly or invisibly?'

Naturally the audience wishes to see it go visibly.

'Oh, that's simple.'

He places his hand around the knot and slides it down and off the rope.

'The knot is gone, but because you asked to see it go visibly here it is . . .'

He tosses a knot out to the audience! Once the surprise is over the magician ties still another knot in the centre of the rope.

'Now,' he explains, 'if you had asked to see it go invisibly I would have done it in about the same way.'

74

He again places his fist around the knot and slides his hand down and off the rope.

'This time however, when I threw it to you...' he tosses the the knot towards the audience,' . . . it would have been invisible.'

His hand is empty and the knot is gone!

'Now if you would like to know why I was able to fool you that time it was because I used a very special knot that's called a *not knot* . . . and, as you've just learned, a not knot is a knot that's really not a knot at all!'

HOW TO DO IT: You will require a piece of soft clothesline about two feet long. To make it soft soak it in warm water for an hour or two and allow it to dry. This will rinse out the starch which makes it stiff.

Tie a knot in one end of the rope and cut it off after pulling the knot tight. Trim off the ends of the knot with scissors until it is small enough to hide comfortably in your hand.

If you wish to perform the trick as described above, you will also require a card case to hold the rope. You can, however, simply have the rope lying on a table, or in your pocket, to begin.

There is one simple trick you must master. It will require some practice on your part, but it can be learned quickly. Tie a simple single overhand knot right in the centre of the long length of rope. Pull the ends to make the knot smaller, but it should not be made too small. Leave a loop in the centre of the knot about three times larger than your thumb (making this knot the right size is why you must experiment and practice).

Hold the rope by one end to show that the knot is in the centre. Now bring your hand over so your fingers go in front of the knot. At the same time, *slip your thumb into the knot.* This is the secret. Fold your fingers loosely around the knot so it appears that you are holding the knot in your clenched fist. (See illustration overleaf.)

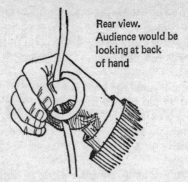

Rear view.
Audience would be
looking at back
of hand

Next, holding the end tightly with your other hand, slide your fist down the rope and off the bottom. If you are doing it properly the knot will unwind around your thumb and actually move down the rope. When your thumb comes off the end, the knot will automatically untie itself and your hand will be left empty.

If anybody tries to duplicate your trick, he will fail. Because he will not know your trick of slipping the thumb inside, and the knot will simply tighten as he moves his fist down.

The extra knot you cut off earlier is hidden in your pocket. After tying a knot in the length of rope and showing it, ask your audience whether they would like to see it vanish 'visibly or invisibly'. As you do this, reach into your pocket with your free hand and remove the hidden knot. Hold it inside your hand. Use this hand to slide the knot off the rope and toss it to the audience. Naturally they receive the knot you have hidden in your hand.

If you practice this just a bit you will soon find it easy to hide the knot in your hand and slip the rope knot at the same time. You can also reach into your pocket to obtain the extra knot without worrying. Remember that nobody knows what you are going to do until the very surprising ending.

To make the knot vanish invisibly is, of course, the easiest part of all. Just slip the knot down the rope and off the end and pretend to hold it in your hand. Pretend to throw it towards the audience and some people will swear they saw the knot vanish right in thin air.

There are many different kinds of vanishing tricks. You will recognize them in other parts of this book. Often you will find a vanish is just one part of a more complicated trick. Some tricks will use a vanish, appearance, penetration, force, and other kinds of trick working together. Because they are arranged to work so well together, the audience will feel it sees just a single trick. These combination tricks certainly demand more work on the magician's part but are most baffling for the viewer. The magician simply gives them too many puzzles to solve at the same time. By studying some chapters you may discover other ideas and tools that you can combine to create more tricks of your own. Magicians who copy others are simply doing tricks. Magicians who devise new tricks or new combinations of tricks are really making magic.

To do this requires some hard work and thought on your part. To be a good magician looks like fun, can be fun, but you will have to work hard at it. Each tool the workman adds makes his work a bit better and easier. Each tool, like the vanish, that the magician adds helps him in the same way.

CHAPTER 8

TRANSFORMATIONS AND TRANSPOSITIONS – CHANGING MAGIC

Another amazing stage trick is called the *Substitution Trunk*. It has been performed by famous magicians all over the world for many years. Sometimes it is called the 'Fastest Trick in the World' because it appears to be all over before anyone realizes what is going to happen. If you are ever fortunate enough to see it done, it will probably go like this:

A girl is placed in a large cloth bag which is tied at the top.

She is then lifted into a large trunk which is examined, closed and locked by members of the audience. The magician then steps on top of the trunk and holds a large cloth in front of him so that only his head shows.

'Ladies and gentlemen, I would like to show you the quickest trick ever invented. Watch closely while I count to ten. One, two, three, four . . .,' he raises the cloth up to hide his head, 'five, . . .' suddenly his voice changes to that of a girl, 'six, seven, eight, nine, TEN!' The cloth drops and the girl is standing on top of the trunk. The trunk is quickly opened the bag removed and untied. The magician steps out!

It is easy to understand why this is a favourite trick. The secret, as with most magic tricks, is very simple, but once it is known the fun and surprise vanish. For this reason, together with the fact that the equipment is much too expensive for the beginner, the substitution trunk must be left as an unexplained mystery for you to ponder.

This kind of trick, however, represents another of the special tools a magician uses. He would call this kind of trick a *transposition*: two objects seem to change places. In the same category he would place *transformations*: one object seems to change into another.

These two types of trick have very big names, but they are parts of a very special vocabulary you will want to learn if you are to become a magician. (By the way, magicians sometimes call themselves *prestidigitators*, and the magic they do *legerdemain*. Perhaps they like big words?)

To understand the difference between a transformation and a transposition, let's learn a trick with each of them.

You might suspect that one object transforming to another would always be a very mysterious, serious, kind of trick. Sometimes, however, you can use a transformation for a bit of comedy. Here is a trick to try when you have some adults in the audience.

LET ME SHOW YOU A NEW TRICK

'I would like to borrow a pound note. I promise that I will not injure it in any way, and I promise that I will give it back in just a few minutes.'

The magician borrows a pound from an adult. He folds it over several times until it is a small bundle. Removing a handkerchief, he places the bundle under it. The corners of the handkerchief hang down and the note is held, through the cloth, at the centre.

'I would like to show you a new trick I have been learning. It's called the *Vanishing Pound Note* trick. You all watched me fold the note and place it under the handkerchief. Let me show you that it is still there.'

A corner of the handkerchief is lifted so that everyone can see the folded note underneath. The corner is released so the note is again hidden.

'Now watch the note vanish. It will go when I say three. One ... two ... three!'

A corner of the handkerchief is pulled and the cloth

opened out. The magician waves the handkerchief as though the note has vanished ... but it hasn't. The folded note flies out of the cloth and drops on to the floor. The audience laughs. The magician is a little embarrassed. He slowly, sheepishly, picks up the folded note and hands it back to the person who loaned it.

'I'm sorry. I told you it was a new trick and I certainly need to practice it more ... Let me show you another trick that I know better ...'

The magician forgets all about his mis-adventure with the note and begins to perform another trick. Naturally people are still laughing at him, and he seems a little shaken by his failure. What's the trick here?

Suddenly the person who loaned the pound lets out a holler. It seems he has opened the folded note to put it back in his wallet, but has discovered it is not a note at all. It is a folded piece of green paper!

'Perhaps you would like to exchange that worthless piece of paper for this more valuable one?' asks the magician as he reaches into his pocket and removes the real pound note.

So, after everyone has had a good laugh at his clumsiness, it is the magician himself who leaves them with a real magical puzzle, and has the last laugh himself.

HOW TO DO IT: Cut a sheet of green paper to a size about the same as a pound note. Fold it into a small package and place it in the middle of your handkerchief, gather the corners together and push it into your pocket.

Borrow a pound note from a spectator and fold it into a bundle which looks something like the one hidden in the handkerchief. Reach into your pocket and take out the handkerchief. Grip the folded green paper bundle through the cloth so that when you take it from your pocket the four corners will be hanging down and the bundle is hidden underneath.

Show the real pound note bundle with your other hand

and poke it up under the handkerchief. When it is under the cloth, hide the real note in your hand and take it right back out, leaving the paper still underneath.

Explain that you have put the note under the handkerchief and, as you are talking, place the hand in your pocket and drop the real note inside. If anyone notices you doing this just lift a corner of the cloth to show the 'note' still there.

You can show the note under the handkerchief because, from a short distance, the green paper will look just like a real pound. Show it quickly, but be sure everyone sees it there. Finally drop the corners of the handkerchief and pretend to make the note vanish. Let it fall to the floor. Pick it up slowly. Be embarrassed. Let the audience laugh at you. Apologize. Be a GOOD ACTOR.

After your fun, be sure to return the original bill to the lender. If your audience is going to have fun, they must learn to trust you and to know that you will always make things right.

If you show two different objects, put them in two different places, then cause each to appear where the other should be you are presenting a transposition (*trans* means change, *position* means place). The two objects don't change in any way, they simply exchange places. Here is a grand transposition you might wish to learn:

TIN AND GLASS: DOUBLE-CROSS

The magician has two separate tables. On one rests a small drinking glass and a paper tube. On the other, a tin of lemonade or beer and a paper tube. He places the tubes over the glass and the tin and waves his hand. When the tubes are removed, the tin is found under the one that held the glass and the glass is discovered under the one which covered the tin a moment before.

Not content with having them change places once, the

magician offers to make them do it again. Once more he covers the tin and the glass with their tubes, and again they mysteriously change places when the tubes are lifted. The audience is more intrigued than ever.

He offers to do it one more time. He covers the tin with the tube and walks towards the other table holding the glass. While he is busy covering the glass with its tube his assistant sneaks on to the stage. The assistant tip-toes to the other table, lifts the tube and sneaks the tin off and into his pocket. He places the tube back on the table and, with a wink towards the audience, he quietly tip-toes from the stage.

The magician, apparently not having seen his assistant's antics, continues along with the trick. He waves his hands and walks towards the table holding the now empty tube.

'Over here we have the tin,' he says, lifting the tube ... and sure enough the stolen tin has reappeared! He picks up the tin and returns to the tube on the other table. When he lifts this tube he finds the glass underneath.

Having completed the trick, and surprised his audience, he proceeds to use a tin opener to open the tin and pour himself a drink!

HOW TO DO IT: You will require quite a few props for this trick. You can find or make them all very easily. You will need three lemonade tins all exactly alike. Two of them are prepared by *removing* the *bottoms* with a tin opener and leaving the tops untouched. The third tin is left full and unprepared.

You will need two identical glasses, plastic ones will work well and even paper cups can be used. They must be small enough to fit inside the empty tins with plenty of room around the sides.

Finally, you must make two paper tubes. They should be prepared from fairly heavy paper. Roll the paper around the tin and allow it to open slightly. Tape or glue the edges, inside and out, to make a tube that fits loosely over the tins.

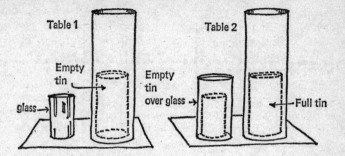

The height of the tubes is important. They should be slightly longer than the height of two tins stacked one on top of another.

To perform the trick you will also need two tables, and an assistant, and both you and your assistant will require a bit of practice.

Set up for the trick in this way: On one table place one empty tube and drop in one of the bottomless tins, open-end down. Place a glass beside the tube. On the other table place a tube with the full tin of lemonade inside it. Beside this tube place a glass and drop the bottomless tin over this glass so it is hidden inside.

Begin the trick at the table with the glass showing. Pick up the tube and drop it over the glass. You should squeeze the sides of the tube as you lift so the hidden tin stays inside. It appears that you have simply covered the glass with a tube, but you have actually hidden it inside a tin.

Walk to the other table. Lift the second tube, squeezing it to hold the full tin inside, and drop it over the tin showing on the table. As you drop the tube, release your grip and the tube will slip down over the lower tin, leaving the full one balanced on top. To the audience it appears you have simply covered a tin with a tube.

An x-ray view through both tubes, at this point, would look like this:

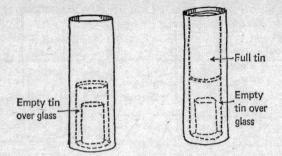

Empty tin over glass

Full tin

Empty tin over glass

Wave your hand a bit as though causing the glass and tin to change places invisibly. Lift the first tube, without squeezing, to show the tin there now. Place the tube down beside it. Lift the second tube, squeezing it towards the bottom so both tins stay inside, showing the glass here. Set the tube down beside the glass.

It appears that you have caused the tin and the glass to change places. Now you must do it again. Simply place the first (empty) tube back over the tin. Squeeze the second tube to keep the tins inside, and place it over the glass.

Make your magic waves over the two tubes and, by simply reversing the above directions it is easy to make the glass appear back under the first tube and the tin back under the second. Release your grip very gently to let the full tin on the second table slide down inside the tube and on to the table. If you release it too quickly it will make a 'thump' and tell everyone there's something inside that 'empty' tube. (Both you and your assistant must practise this carefully.)

Now you must offer to do it one more time, 'for the people in the back who weren't watching closely enough.' Return to the second table, which now has the tin showing. Squeeze the tube to keep the full tin inside and place it over the empty tin as in the first transposition. Start to walk towards the other table.

While you are replacing the tube and empty tin over the

glass on the first table it is time for your assistant to sneak in! His job is most important. The assistant squeezes the tube at the top so the full tin stays inside and places it down to one side of the tin on the table, releasing his grip gently as you had to do.

Once the tube is set on the table he *slides* the exposed tin off (remember that it has a glass hidden inside) and on to the palm of his hand. His palm will prevent the glass from falling out. Then he simply pushes the tube back in place and sneaks off with the tin in his hand.

He must do all of these things as quickly as possible, while your back is turned. You must practise this together to have it work properly.

Once your assistant has left, and the audience thinks they know something you don't, you are ready to return to the table and lift the tube to discover the 'stolen' tin underneath. Naturally, now this will be the full tin. It's a nice touch now to crumple up the tube or merely show it is empty just to confuse anyone who thinks they know how you did it.

Pick up the full tin and return to the first table. Squeeze the tube on this table to keep the tin inside. Lift the tube to show the glass and set the tube, with its hidden tin, aside. Now you're all set to reach into your pocket for a tin opener . . . open the lemonade . . . pour yourself a drink . . . and fool anybody who guesses that you were really using two tins and two glasses!

There are many other transformation and transposition tricks. Perhaps you will find others elsewhere in this book. Often a magician creates one by combining a vanish with an appearance trick. If one object vanishes and another appears in its place it appears as a transformation. Perhaps, with a little thought, you might be able to create your own 'changing magic' trick?

CHAPTER 9

PENETRATIONS – SOLID THROUGH SOLID

If I threw a baseball at a window and instead of breaking the glass the ball passed right through without causing any damage at all, would you be surprised?

Your reaction to the idea of this happening will be the same as the audience's when the magician shows them a trick called a *penetration*. Like many magic tricks, a penetration surprises the audience because it seems scientifically impossible. If you can do something that 'just can't happen', then you must be a magician. A penetration trick appears to be just that . . . something that just can't happen.

A simple description of a penetration trick would be an illusion of a solid object passing through another solid object with neither object being harmed in any way. Actually, there are a number of different ways this could be presented. The audience might see each as a different trick, but to the magician they are all basic penetrations. Here are some different ways they might be performed.

1 A rope wrapped around your body is suddenly pulled through. (A basic penetration.)
2 The ends of a string are held and you cause a ring to become threaded on it. (Almost the reverse of the above.)
3 A pencil is pushed through a sheet of paper but, when removed, the paper is quite whole. (Mutilating an object without causing any damage.)

There are many other forms that penetrations can take, and you will find others in this book that you will recognize. For now, however, let's consider just a few of them using those ideas listed above. You might begin with a simple penetration . . . just passing one object through another.

THE COIN THROUGH THE CLOTH

The magician spreads a handkerchief flat on the table and lays a coin in the centre on top of the cloth. He rolls the handkerchief over and into a tube, and then unrolls it. The coin is no longer in the centre, but when he lifts the handkerchief the coin is found underneath.

Did the coin actually penetrate the handkerchief? It certainly looks as though it did . . . but that's impossible, isn't it?

HOW TO DO IT: Study the illustrations carefully as you read the directions and actually try this trick. You will discover this is the easiest way to understand how it happens. When you do it properly it will practically happen by itself.

Spread a handkerchief flat on a table so one corner is facing directly towards you. Place a coin in the centre, but just a bit *closer to the corner facing you* than the diagonal corner. Fold the diagonal corner (away from you) over the

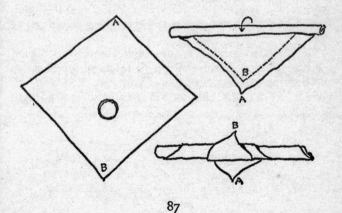

coin and down over the corner closest to you. Be sure this corner overlaps the bottom one a bit (this will happen if your coin was slightly towards you to start with).

Now, beginning in the middle where the coin is, roll the handkerchief towards you into a tube. If you are doing this as you read, and you have overlapped the corners properly, you will discover a corner suddenly appears in the centre of the rolled up handkerchief. Take hold of this corner with one hand, and the one still flat on the table with the other, pull them apart. The handkerchief will unroll and the trick is done ... you will find the handkerchief is now *over* the coin.

If you spend a few minutes playing with this trick you will quickly catch on to how and why it works even though it sounds very complicated. The first time it happens properly you may find yourself surprised. Remember this surprise because it is the same surprise your audience will have the first time they see it. Once you learn this simple penetration you will enjoy doing it because it practically works right.

Perhaps the most famous penetration is *Sawing A Woman In Half*. A girl is placed in a wooden box with her head and feet extending out the ends and the magician cuts her in half with a huge lumber saw. Naturally, at the end, this penetration becomes a restoration and everything comes out all itself.

The beginner certainly cannot duplicate this very elaborate stage illusion; however the penetration of a person can certainly be part of your show if you wish. You won't require a box or a saw, but you will use a person and a length of rope.

MY FRIEND WITHOUT A MIDDLE

The magician introduces his assistant, and explains a bit about the famous trick called *Sawing A Lady In Half*. He asks the audience if they would like to know how this trick is done.

'It's very simple,' explains the magician. 'All the magician has to do is to find an assistant who was born without a middle! Naturally, if he doesn't have a middle then a saw, or anything else, can pass right between the top and bottom without causing any damage at all.'

The audience laughs, but the magician continues by introducing his helper who, he explains, is one of those rare people born without a middle.' He offers to prove it.

Taking a piece of rope, he wraps it around his assistant's waist and ties it with a knot in the front. He hands the ends to two spectators and instructs them:

'Now, on the count of three pull hard and quickly on the ends of the rope.'

He counts, they pull, and the rope seems to melt right through the assistant's middle, leaving only the knot still tied in the centre of the rope.

HOW TO DO IT: You require only two things for this trick and one, naturally is NOT an assistant without a middle! You will, however, need an assistant and he should be a boy ... wearing a pair of trousers! You will also require a piece of clothesline about ten feet long. (Some magicians like to use a piece of coloured ribbon instead.) You will also need an audience that is not sitting beside or behind you!

If you study the illustration on the following page you can see just how the rope is wrapped around the boy. You will notice that it really doesn't go around him at all. You can practice on yourself to learn just how to wrap the rope.

Begin with your assistant facing towards the audience and

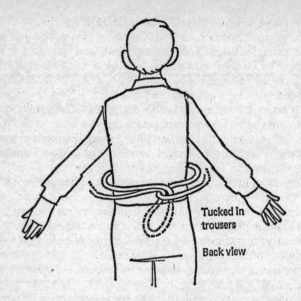

Tucked in trousers

Back view

place the centre of the rope against his stomach. Toss the two ends of the rope around each side of him. Step around the boy and draw the rope tightly around his waist.

While you are behind your assistant, and the audience can't see your hands, you simply form a loop in one rope. Wrap this loop around the rope coming around the other side, and tuck the loop down inside the back of his trousers. You can then bring the ends back around his waist. Actually, it appears that you have made a loop around the boy, but you have just arranged each rope so it goes half-way around and then back to the front. The loop down his trousers holds the secret in place!

Tie a knot in front of his waist with the two ends. This should be a simple, single, overhand knot . . . nothing fancy, please.

Invite two spectators up to assist you. Have one stand on

each side of the boy. Be sure they are slightly in front of him so they can't look behind and get a glimpse of the loop in the rope. Hand each of them one end of the rope and count to three.

When they pull, the loop will come out of your assistant's trousers and the rope will be free of his waist. The knot, however, will remain in the rope in the form of a big loop. The audience will believe this loop was the same loop that was, only a moment ago, encircling the boy. The only explanation is that the rope passed through him ... or, perhaps, he really doesn't have a middle to get in the way?

Thus far you have used only unprepared objects plus your own nerve to convince your audience that you can indeed cause solid objects to pass through one another. Perhaps now you might like to make your job easier, and perhaps even your tricks more baffling, by using another special tool available to the magician ... the gimmick. By using a piece of apparatus that the audience does not know exists, you have them at a considerable disadvantage and your tricks will look more like real magic. Here is a penetration that has been used by many magicians for many years, but to someone who has never seen it, it appears absolutely impossible.

THE RING ON THE STRING

The magician shows three objects: a piece of string with a big sewing needle on the end, a round circle of coloured paper, and a plain white envelope.

The inside of the envelope is shown to be quite empty. The envelope is folded flat and the needle is pushed into one side and out the other, thus threading the envelope on the centre of the string. A spectator is invited to hold the ends of the string.

Opening the envelope, the magician drops the disc of coloured paper inside. He seals the envelope.

He lets the envelope hang from the string being held by the

spectator and asks the assistant to swing the envelope back and forth. When this is being done the magician recites a strange chant as he waves his hands over the envelope.

'Coloured disc in your envelope swing,
Thread yourself upon the string!'

With the helper still holding the ends of the string, the magician then reaches down and grasps the envelope. He tears off one end and still keeping a firm grasp on the envelope instructs the helper to pull hard on the ends of the string. The string tears down the envelope and out the end. As it comes free the audience will be very surprised to find that the disc of paper is threaded nicely in the middle!

HOW TO DO IT: Surprisingly, if you're trying to guess the gimmick in this trick, there are two things the audience doesn't know about. One, naturally is a duplicate disc of paper. Both discs should fit easily inside the envelope and they should match exactly. They do *not* have holes in the centre.

The second gimmick, you have guessed, is the envelope. It is not quite as plain as it appears, but it is very easy to prepare. You will need two envelopes of the same size. Cut

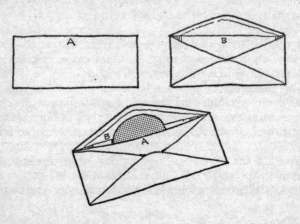

one along all the edges, and cut off the flap to obtain the plain white front. Trim the edges of this so that it will *just* slip inside the other envelope.

Place one of your coloured paper discs inside the plain envelope.

Apply a little paste to the top and bottom edges of the envelope front you prepared earlier. Drop this sheet into the envelope, over the coloured disc so that it is pasted to the front of the plain envelope and the coloured disc is between. Squeeze the envelope and press it along the edges, be careful not to paste the disc, then set it aside to dry. When this envelope is opened it should appear quite ordinary.

The string you use should be heavy and strong. Obtain a large needle from your mother to use with this string. If she doesn't have a large, dramatic-looking one, you can purchase an upholstery needle from any store that sells sewing supplies. The needle does not have to be very sharp.

To work the trick, simply show the inside of the envelope. Thanks to the secret flap it will appear empty. Push the needle through the sides. Actually you thread the hidden disc on to the string at this time but the audience doesn't really know what you are going to do yet.

Show the original disc of coloured paper to your audience and place it into the envelope. Your assistant, who is now holding the ends of the string, will have to slacken his grip to allow you to do this, but remind him to 'hold the ends tightly'. Push this disc down towards one end of the envelope, even if you have to crunch it up a bit to get it away from the string.

Seal the envelope and instruct your helper to make it swing back and forth. Recite your magic incantation. It works best if you wink at your audience while you are saying it and pretend to be very serious!

Tear the *end* off the envelope opposite the end where you placed the original disc. Squeeze the other end of the envelope (and the disc hidden inside) and ask your assistant to pull on the string. Turn the end of the envelope, with the torn off end, towards him as he pulls. The string will tear its way out of the envelope and pull the duplicate disc threaded on it out of its secret compartment.

Crumple up the envelope and drop it in your pocket or set it in some safe place. Don't leave it where prying eyes will find it.

Another famous stage illusion represents still another type of penetration. It is called the *Sword Box*. It is usually a small box, just large enough to hold a person. After placing his assistant in the box, the magician proceeds to push dozens of sharp swords through the box at every angle. Soon the box resembles a pincushion and it is impossible to believe that the assistant inside could avoid looking the same. But, lo when the swords are removed, the assistant pops up looking completely happy about her recent 'operation'.

This sort of penetration is not impossible. It is indeed perfectly possible to push a sword into a person. The magic here is being able to do it without harming anyone. The magician is able to do it differently from anyone else, so it is a trick that is 'impossible' to do the way the magician does.

If you substitute a large envelope for the box, a sheet of paper for the girl assistant, and a table knife for the sword, you can easily present a surprising version of the famous *Sword Box Penetration*.

A STAB IN THE DARK

The magician displays a large manila mailing envelope, a sheet of coloured paper just a bit smaller than the envelope, a table knife and a handkerchief.

He slips the sheet of coloured paper inside the envelope and closes the flap.

'Watch,' he exclaims. 'I will now make a small hole in the centre of the paper by stabbing it right through the envelope.'

He reaches behind the envelope with the knife in his hand while he holds the envelope with his other hand. Suddenly the point of the knife is seen to emerge through the front of the envelope. He continues pushing the knife until it comes all the way through and falls on to the table.

'Just to prove there really is a hole in the paper, watch while I push a handkerchief through it.'

He picks up the handkerchief by one corner and moves it behind the envelope. A moment later the corner pokes through the hole. He reaches in front and draws the handkerchief all the way through.

'But,' explains the magician, 'just like the magician's assistant who enters a small box and has hundreds of swords pushed through her ...'

The magician opens the flap of the envelope and draws out the sheet of paper.

'... our paper comes out whole, er that is ... I should say it comes out with *no* hole at all!'

HOW TO DO IT: You must prepare your envelope by making a slit about half-way down the back side. The slit should extend all the way across the back.

When the paper is slipped into the envelope it goes in the

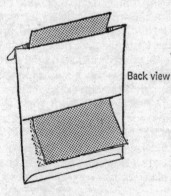

Back view

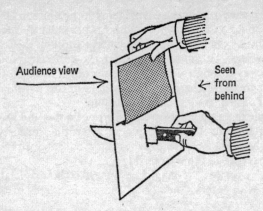

Audience view → ← Seen from behind

top, but *out the centre slit*. The bottom of the paper simply hangs outside the envelope. As long as the audience sees only the front side, they will feel certain that you have just slid the paper into the envelope and closed the flap. Note: By gluing the lower half of the envelope, under the slit, to the plain front it will be impossible to slip the paper all the way down inside the envelope. This will make it much easier to push it out of the slit smoothly.

When you reach behind the envelope with the knife, you naturally reach up under the paper and push the knife through. If you make a little hole in the front of the envelope before starting the trick, you will find it is much easier to push the knife through during your performance. The handkerchief is pushed through in the same manner.

Some magicians find it is much easier to push the knife or handkerchief through if they first reach behind and bend the flap of paper up and catch it with their thumb holding the top of the envelope. Whichever method turns out to be the easier for you is the one to use.

Many magic tricks require you to 'watch your angles', that is, remember not to allow your audience to be seated too far to either side. This trick has very bad angles and you must watch them carefully. If anyone is able to glimpse beside the envelope they will see the paper being folded upwards. It is a fine trick for a few friends, or on a stage, but might be a hard one to do at a birthday party where people are sitting everywhere and any tricks with 'angles' are practically impossible.

If you saw a magician perform this trick, would you recognize it as a penetration? As you watch a magician perform it is not important to try to figure out how his tricks work. The beginner, however, is very wise in trying to identify what *kind* of trick he is watching. Recognizing penetrations, vanishes, appearances, tranformatons and the rest ... and seeing how many magicians put them together, and how many of each he does, will be one of the most important things you can learn from him when it comes time for you to put your own show together.

Here, for example, are three stage illusions:

In the guillotine trick the same blade that chops a cabbage in two passes harmlessly through a girl's neck.
A pretty girl is placed inside a huge cannon which is fired at a glass box. The girl suddenly appears inside.
A ribbon is tied to a bullet which is loaded into a pistol. A girl stands in front of a target and the magician fires at her. The bullet, with the ribbon goes through her into the target and the magician pulls the ribbon back and forth through the girl's middle.

If you saw these tricks in a magic show, would you now recognize that they are all penetrations? Would you also realize that, because the girl is always 'made right again' they are also a kind of restoration? Once you find yourself watching a magician and thinking this way, rather than just, 'Oh, I know how he does that,' you are well on your way to becoming a magician yourself ... at least you are proving that you do really want to be a magician.

CHAPTER 10

RESTORATIONS – ALL TOGETHER AGAIN

Have you ever heard the expression, 'Give a person enough rope and he'll hang himself'? Magicians have given a twist to this old saying: 'If you give a magician enough rope he will probably just cut it in half.' This is actually a joke about one of the oldest kinds of magic trick – restorations.

If you ever broke a window pane or ripped your trousers accidentally, you have probably wished you could some-how put the pieces back together again. This, naturally would be impossible and therefore it should not surprise you that a magician would try to make a trick out of it. To a magician a restoration is simply the destruction of some object, then its restoration to its former condition. To the magician this is just a basic trick, and certainly not at all impossible. His job, after all, is to do the impossible.

Our joke about the magician cutting his rope in half comes from the fact that the trick of cutting and restoring a rope is one of the oldest magic tricks. Every magician has his favourite method and there are hundreds of ways to ac-complish this 'miracle'. Here is a very simple method you may like because it is very surprising to see.

CONFUSING YOUR AUDIENCE
BY SHOWING HOW IT'S DONE

'Some magicians allow themselves to be securely tied with ropes and in a flash they escape as though they had simply passed through them like a cloud,' explains the magician.

'I would like to give you a simple demonstration. Many people have asked me how this rope trick is possible, and I do think this demonstration will help you to understand. I will not bother to tie myself up completely, but just one loop around my waist will make it clear.'

He takes a six-foot length of rope and wraps one end around his waist. He ties this end securely to the middle of the rope to form a tight loop about his middle.

'Now,' he explains, 'you will notice that I cannot escape from this rope simply by pulling on it because the knot holds it tightly in place.'

He tugs hard against the free end of the rope.

'Assuming I was completely tied, I would probably step behind a screen or into a closet for a few moments and step out completely untied. Most people wonder what happens inside that screen or closet and this is what I would like to show you. Imagine that I have hidden myself from your view . . . hidden in my pocket I have a pair of scissors . . .'

The magician picks up a pair of scissors and shows them to the audience.

' . . . which I use to simply snip the rope free.'

The magician cuts the rope off just beside the knot and removes the rope from his waist. He holds it up by one end so the audience can see it tied with a knot in the centre.

'Unfortunately,' explains the magician, 'I am left with two pieces of rope still tied together with the knot. Naturally I cannot walk out with the rope like this because everyone would know that I have simply cut the rope to escape. So before leaving my closet I simply coil the rope around my hand . . .'

The magician does this with the knotted rope.

' . . . and cause the knot to vanish and the two separate pieces of rope become one again.'

He uncoils the rope from his hand and shows it is a single unknotted piece. The knot has vanished. He tosses the rope out into the audience to be examined.

'And now,' explains the magician, 'that you know the secret of the rope escape trick, I hope that you will keep it our secret and never . . . never . . . tell anyone else!'

HOW TO DO IT: This is actually one of the easiest rope tricks. It almost works itself, but you should practice it several times before showing anyone. You will require only a pair of scissors and a piece of rope about six feet long.

Magicians use special rope for their tricks. It is soft and very flexible. You can buy this magic rope at a magic or joke shop, but regular clothesline will work well if you prepare it. Soak it for about an hour or two in water and dry it out. This soaking will remove the starch which is responsible for the rope's stiffness and will leave the rope much softer. Now it will be easier to handle and to cut. The story you tell should be similar to the one you just read.

Begin by wrapping the rope around your waist. Tie one end to the middle of the rope. If you tie the rope in this manner, and you use simple overhand knots, it will always make a slip knot. (The only way to understand why this is true is actually to try it with a length of rope.)

When you cut the knot off with your scissors, cut the end you tied to the centre. This way you will actually have a single long length of rope with a short-piece knotted around the middle. If you cut the wrong side you will really have two pieces knotted together and this is *not* what you want.

It is a good idea to snip off the two ends of the knot to make them as short as possible. This will give you a smaller knot that will be easier to handle later on.

When you have cut the rope properly, and have told your audience that, 'I am left with two pieces of rope tied together with the knot,' they will believe you. They can see the knot and it appears that you are simply telling them what they already see.

To 'restore' the rope, hold one end in your left hand and coil the rest of it around your right. When you reach the knot, continue coiling and the knot will slide down the rope (inside your left hand) and right off the end. You will be left with the rope coiled around your right hand, while the knot remains securely hidden inside the left. Grasp the free end of the rope with your left hand and pull the rope off your right. Show your audience that the rope is once again a single piece and toss it out for them to examine. While they are looking at the rope you will have plenty of time to drop the

Knot →

knot into your pocket or on to the table when you reach for your next trick.

An even more startling restoration can be done with a strip of paper. Imagine cutting a piece right out of the centre of a narrow piece of paper ... the audience actually sees this piece fall to the floor ... and yet when the strip is shown a moment later it is once again a single piece. This trick requires a bit of gimmicking on your part, but you will be repaid by the gasp of surprise you will receive.

WHO NEEDS A MIDDLE?

Showing a strip of paper, the magician explains:

'Do you realize that the most important parts of a strip of paper like this are the two ends? After all ...' as he points to each end in turn, '... one end must always be here ... and the other end here.' The magician points to the two ends and says, 'The ends couldn't really be anywhere else, could they? But the middle is not really important at all. What is the middle anyway? It's just a place somewhere between the two ends, usually the centre but it could really be anywhere ... it all depends on where the two ends are. As a matter of fact ...' he explains as he folds the paper strip in half and reaches for a pair of scissors, '... we can cut the middle right out of a strip of paper.' He clips the centre from the paper and it falls to the floor, 'and most important ... because we still have the two ends, and they're the most important, we must still have a middle half-way between them ... right?'

The magician opens the paper strip out, showing that it is still one piece.

HOW TO DO IT: Perhaps the very best part of this trick is the silly talk you give to explain why it happens. It is actually a quick trick that will require very little practice on your part. The dialogue will make it even more fun for your audience.

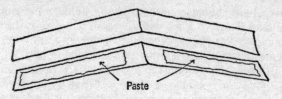

Paste

Any kind of paper can be used. A strip cut from newspaper is perfect. Actually, you will require *two* strips about one inch wide and eighteen inches in length. You will also need a little glue or paste.

Fold both of the paper strips in half to find the exact middles. In spite of your explanation, the middle is really the most important part for this trick to work properly. Begin applying paste to one strip about one inch from the centre fold. Put paste on it from this point to the end. Do the same on the other end, again starting about one inch to one side of the centre fold. Now carefully lay the other strip of paper on top and press the two together. When you are done you should have two strips pasted together except for two inches in the middle. Allow them to dry.

When the strips are dry, fold them by opening out the unpasted centres. One strip is folded up, and the other down.

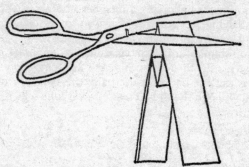

Now, hold the strip opened out by holding the ends in each hand. The two strips will appear as one. This is the way it is displayed to your audience.

In performing the trick the strip is folded in half. As you do this you secretly fold the inside centre strip down. The part folded down is hidden by the paper strips on the sides. Your hand holds this lower fold which further hides the extra strip. The part sticking up above your hand, the extra centre is the 'middle' that is cut off with the scissors.

After cutting, as you remove the paper strip from your hand, turn it over. Open it out and the audience will see the full length of paper, thanks to the extra strip pasted on the back. They will assume this is the original strip which has somehow become restored.

Once the trick is done, crumple up the paper and drop it into your pocket. This way nobody will be able to find the strip later and discover the secret to its preparation. Do this trick quickly, and then proceed to your next trick. If you show off too long someone might ask you to turn the strip over, which of course, you can't do. Unlike the rope in the above trick, you cannot pass this strip for examination. Therefore, it is far better to surprise your audience and to move along into another trick while they are still puzzling over it.

Still another restoration might appeal to you even more. Can you imagine allowing a member of the audience to do the destroying, yet still allowing you to perform the restoration? The way in which you do this sounds equally impossible: you simply show him one thing, let him break another one just like it, then show him the first one and convince him it is the one he broke. Actually this is a very old trick but you will find that it still amazes everyone who sees it for the first time.

MATCH-ING MATCH TRICK

The magician shows a handkerchief and a wooden match to the audience. Then he drops the match into the folds of a handkerchief and gathers the cloth around it. He invites a member of the audience to feel the match through the handkerchief. Actually, several people in the audience could participate. Finally, he asks one of them to break it in half and in half again.

Once the spectator is convinced the match is really broken, the magician lifts the handkerchief by one corner and, as he says the 'magic word' (how about 'match-ic?') the match falls on to the table. It is completely restored and may be examined carefully. The handkerchief is spread out and shown on both sides.

HOW TO DO IT: Two wooden kitchen matches and one large handkerchief are all that you will require. The handkerchief must be carefully chosen however. It must be one with a large hem on the outside edge.

One end of the handkerchief hem is probably open. If it is not, a quick snip with a pair of scissors will cut enough threads to allow it to be opened enough to slip a match in. Push one of the matches into the hem until it is completely hidden inside.

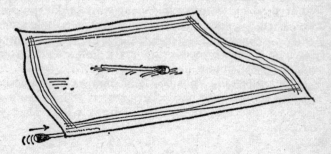

To perform the trick, simply show the handkerchief freely. No one will be aware of the hidden match. Also show the duplicate match. Lay the handkerchief flat on the table and place the duplicate match in the centre. Pick up the corner of the handkerchief near the match hidden in the hem and lay it directly over the visible match. Next fold in the other corners and finally gather the handkerchief into a sort of ball. You can actually be quite clumsy with this, in fact, by being somewhat clumsy nobody will suspect you are doing anything but wrapping a match in a handkerchief.

Ask someone to feel the match through the cloth. Be sure you hold the handkerchief and make certain it is the match in the hem they feel. Still holding the handkerchief, ask him to break the match, then break it a second time.

When this has been done you simply have to shake the handkerchief open to show the match restored (because it was never broken). Quickly show the handkerchief empty on both sides and place it into your pocket as you invite the audience to examine the 'restored' match carefully.

There is a very basic idea used by magicians for restoration types of tricks in this match routine. The easiest way to restore a destroyed object is, often, simply to substitute a similar-looking object for it. If the substituted object looks exactly the same, the audience will see it as the original one. How to exchange one object for another is the real trick, and magicians have discovered many ways of doing it secretly. Using this idea it is easy to see that it really doesn't matter how badly you seem to destroy the original object . . . in fact, the more you mutilate it, the more wondrous the restoration will appear.

There are actually a number of different ways a magician can fool his audience into believing he is able to cause a destroyed object to be restored. Two you have already learned:

1 Cutting or destroying only a small part of the object, but causing people to think that the damage was much more serious.
2 Actually destroying the object, but substituting a matching object for it and convincing the audience that it is the original.

There is another method you might like to investigate.

3 Convincing the audience that an object has been damaged while actually it is not harmed in any way.

Without method number three it would be quite impossible for a stage magician to perform one of his most famous illusions: *Cutting A Woman In Half*. Naturally the magician cannot cut a real woman up and substitute another for her, nor can he even cut a small part of her, so method number three is the only answer to this mystery. This trick is far too complicated for the beginner. However you can do a similar trick which actually works on somewhat the same principle.

CUTTING ONE PAPER DOLL IN TWO

A cut-out drawing of a girl is shown and passed out for the audience to examine. A sealed envelope is shown and the ends are cut off. The paper doll is returned and placed into the envelope so that the audience can see her head poking out one end and her feet out the other.

Taking his scissors, the magician places them around the envelope and neatly snips it in half through the centre. Apparently the doll is cut in half also.

Holding the separate ends of the envelope together he waves the scissors over them three times. He then reaches towards the doll's head and draws her free from the envelope pieces. She is completely restored and appears none the worse for her experience even when carefully examined.

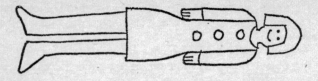

HOW TO DO IT: You will require only an envelope, a pair of scissors and a paper doll that fits inside the envelope. You should draw the doll on a sheet of heavy paper and cut her out. Your doll might look like the one in the illustration, however she must be the correct size for the envelope you will use. She must be thin enough to slip comfortably inside, and long enough so her head and feet will stick out the ends. The envelope too, must be specially fixed for the performance. Seal the envelope and cut two slits in the back about an inch on each side of the middle. When the audience sees the envelope be certain to keep this side away from them.

During the performance simply snip off each end of the envelope and slip the doll inside. Actually you must thread the doll in one end of the envelope, out the first slit, back inside at the second slit, and out the opposite end of the envelope. As long as your audience sees only the front side of the envelope it will appear that you have simply pushed the doll in one end and out the other.

You are then able to cut the envelope in half, but not the doll, by slipping one blade of the scissors between the doll and the envelope and the other blade in front.

Hold the two sections of the envelope together after cutting so nobody catches a glimpse of the girl's middle. Do your magic by waving the scissors three times over the girl. (Some magicians say it really doesn't do anything, but it makes the show look better.) Take hold of the girl's head and give a pull. She will slip out of the envelope, naturally all in one piece and you can show the envelope is indeed in two pieces.

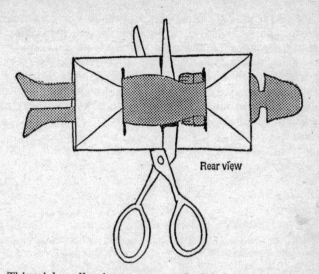

Rear view

This trick really gives you a wonderful chance to make up your own patter. Probably the best patter would be some sort of talk about the famous *Cutting a Lady in Half* illusion, but you might choose to talk about scissors that cut only what you tell them to, or some new way you have discovered to make cuts heal quickly in people. You might also use just a strip of paper, or ribbon, or rope instead of a cutout girl. This would give you different presentations and a chance to create a new trick on your own.

There are still other kinds of restoration trick. When a magician performs a restoration he is simply returning things to normal. Sometimes a restoration is a fine trick all by itself, as are the examples in this section. But often, a restoration is just one part of a more complicated trick. A good trick might consist of a routine made up of a vanish, a force, an appearance, and a restoration. If you study the *Card in The Orange* trick described in the section on *Making the Choice Right*, you will understand how this works.

If you read *Magic by the Book* in the section on *Comedy Magic* you will discover still another way a magician can restore, or make things right.

When the magician presents a penetration (see *Penetrations* section) he is also performing a kind of restoration, that is, fixing one object after passing another through it. Because a restoration is actually impossible, it is a very important part of a magician's repertoire.

CHAPTER 11

SPECIAL MAGIC – SPECIAL MAGICIANS

As you become better known as a magician you will find yourself making friends with other magicians. Most magicians are very friendly and anxious to talk with people who share their interest and are not just trying to find out how the tricks are done.

As you meet other magicians you will be asked what kind of magic interests you most. This does not mean, 'Do you like vanishes or restorations?' These are just basic kinds of tricks. The questions are, 'Do you like small tricks, stage-size tricks, or giant illusions with living people?' Rather than talk about the size of the tricks, however, most magicians have special names for the kinds of magicians they are. If they enjoy small intimate tricks, they are *close-up* magicians. Perhaps with larger tricks they are *stage* or *club* performers. And magicians who do magic with living people and large animals, call themselves *illusionists*. Other special kinds of magicians are *sleight of hand* artists who use small objects and their hands only, *children's magicians* who prefer to entertain young people, and *comedy* magicians who try so hard to be funny that they often don't do a single trick that works correctly.

The beginner is not wise to try to specialize in any single kind of magic. In fact, most professional magicians have tried their hand at all kinds before deciding which they most enjoy.

There are still other very special kinds of magicians. Their tricks are different from the kinds you have read about so far and many people do not think of them as magicians at all. Rather than doing tricks which everyone knows are impossible, these people do things which make others wonder if perhaps they are indeed possible. An example would be mind reading. If you thought of a word and I was able to name it, you might believe that I could read your mind.

These people, who appear to be mind readers, are a very special type of magician. They call themselves *mentalists*. One kind of magician is blindfolded very securely by someone in the audience. Everyone is usually convinced that he could not possibly see. Yet they watch him move around and point to objects as though he could see right through his blindfold. The magician who does this sort of thing calls his act *X-ray Eyes*.

And finally, probably the most well-known magician who doesn't appear to be a magician is the *escapologist*. He enjoys nothing more than being tied securely or locked into something and then trying to escape. Usually, the escapologist uses tricks to aid him. Therefore, he is nothing more than a special kind of a magician.

It is certainly worthwhile to know something about mentalists, escapologists, and X-ray eyes. Even though you may never wish to specialize in these kinds of magic, one or two of these tricks would be something different you could try for your friends.

Here is a very simple mind reading trick.

THINKING ABOUT COLOUR

The mentalist hands four small squares of cloth to a member of the audience. Each square is a different colour and each has a safety pin clippped to it.

He turns his back and asks a spectator to place any one of the cloth squares in his hand and hide the remaining three. When this has been done the mentalist faces his helper, but he keeps the square in his hand, hidden behind his back.

'Please concentrate for a moment on the colour of the cloth you have given me,' says the mentalist. 'Do not think of it by name but simply think of a big square of the actual colour in your mind. Ah, yes, I can see it now ... it is green!'

For the first time he removes his hand holding the square so he can see it and shows that it is indeed the green one. He hands it back to the spectator and allows him to try it again. The magician can repeat this trick as often as he wishes and with anybody who cares to challenge him.

HOW TO DO IT: 'It must be mind reading!' is what you are trying to make your audience say. Therefore, it should not look tricky. You must use plain squares of coloured cloth, all the same size and weight (you'll need four of those) and you must use four safety pins all the same size.

After a few trials your audience will be studying the cloth and pins very carefully to see if they can detect a trick. Only if they decide these objects are unprepared will they think you *might* really be a mind reader.

Yet it is not real mind reading and there is a trick to it. The trick is in the pins. Each pin is prepared in a special manner so you can tell one from another, but the differences should be so slight the audience can't notice them.

You will require a file and a pair of pliers to change the pins. Study the illustration and change them in these ways:

Pin 1 – not changed at all (illustration 1)
Pin 2 – File point flat (illustration 2)
Pin 3 – Bend point slightly inward (illustration 3)
Pin 4 – Bend point slightly outward (illustration 4)

Once these changes have been made, fasten each pin through a corner of the cloth, and remember which pin is in which colour.

As an excuse for having pins in the cloth squares, clip another pin through all of the pins in the cloths.

When you are ready to perform the trick, remove the bundle, open the separate pin and hand out the squares to a

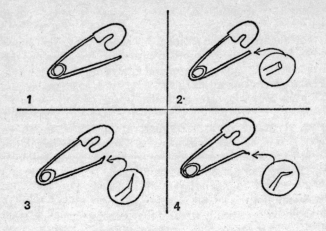

1

2

3

4

spectator. It will appear that the pins are in the squares simply to aid you in keeping them together.

If you wish to make this trick even more elaborate you can use more colours of cloth. Naturally you will have to devise other ways to alter pins to identify them. You might file the tips flat and bend them in, out, or to the side, or you might try filing a tiny notch at different places on the pin. It would be a wonderful trick if you give people a choice of 20 different colours, but it would also be a real mental trick . . . that is, you would have to do a lot of memorizing to know which pin represents which colour.

Also, like many mental tricks, please do not repeat it too many times for the same audience. They will probably never catch on to your secret, but you can be sure they will soon become bored.

If you would truly like to make your audience wonder about your mind reading ability, perhaps the next trick will appeal to you even more. Unlike the last, you can show this one only once.

The mentalist hands a book to a member of the audience and asks that he look through it to assure himself that every page is different and that the book is not prepared in any way.

'Now,' he explains, 'I am going to ask you to think of just one word in that book. I will then attempt to read your mind and name that word. Just so that nobody will suspect that you and I have arranged anything beforehand, however, I am going to ask several other people to help you decide which word you should think of.'

He hands a sheet of blank paper to a member of the audience to call out a number between one and nine. The spectator with the paper writes it down. This is repeated twice more with other people, until finally a number with three digits is on the paper.

'Now please reverse the three numbers and write it on the paper. If the three numbers reversed make a number larger than the one already on the paper please write it above; if it is smaller, write it below. When you have done this, please hand the paper to the person next to you.'

This is done and the spectator who receives the paper is asked to, 'subtract the two numbers ... and hand the sheet to the person next to you.'

The person who next receives the sheet is asked to reverse the three digits produced by the subtraction, and write them under the subtraction. He is then asked to add these two numbers together, and hand the sheet along to another person.

The final person is asked to add all of the digits in this total together and write his final total in big numbers on the sheet. He is asked to draw a circle around the number and hand the sheet to the spectator holding the book.

'Remember,' explains the mentalist, 'I did not know what the first three numbers would be, and I certainly haven't done the arithmetic in my head, nor have I memorized the book you are holding. Would you please turn to the page number written on the sheet and study the first word on that page?'

The spectator turns to the page, and studies the word. After a few moments of 'Mind-reading,' the mentalist gives the correct word even though he has not touched the book, the paper, nor seen the page number since beginning the experiment.

HOW TO DO IT: Take any book or magazine and open it to page 18. Memorize the first word on page 18. This is the word the spectator is going to think of. The question is, how to make him do it. This is not done with magic ... this is done with máthematics!

First, three spectators call out numbers between 1 and 9 and these are written down side by side. This results in a three digit number. You could simply ask for any 3 digit number, but this way has more audience participation and will make your final trick harder to figure out.

Let's, as an example, say 4, 3, 8 have been called to make 438:

$$438$$

The spectator is asked to reverse these numbers (834) and, if it is larger write it over the original number, or if smaller, to write it below. It is larger, so he would write:

$$834$$
$$438$$

The next person is asked to subtract the numbers.

$$834$$
$$438$$
$$\overline{}$$
$$396$$

The next person to get the paper is invited to reverse the numbers in the answer and write them under the total.

$$
\begin{array}{r}
834 \\
-438 \\
\hline
396 \\
693
\end{array}
$$

... and then to add these two together.

$$
\begin{array}{r}
834 \\
-438 \\
\hline
396 \\
+693 \\
\hline
1089
\end{array}
$$

The final person is asked to add all of the numbers in the final total together:

$$1 + 0 + 8 + 9 = 18$$

And 18 is the page on which you memorized the first word.

You might ask what would happen if the first three people did not name 4, 3, and 8? The answer is 'nothing' the trick will still work. If you follow the directions above you can start with any three numbers and you will always finish with 18 being written for the spectator holding the book.

It's not mind reading ... it's arithmetic ... but it's up to you to convince your audience that it's not arithmetic, it's mind reading. You can do this by concentrating very hard while he is looking at the word in the book. Perhaps you can suggest, 'Will you please stop thinking about girls. Is that all you ever have on your mind?' or 'I see a lot of little white things in your head ... oh, excuse me. I was looking at your teeth.' Try to make the audience forget about the arithmetic and believe that they helped choose the word that you are trying to discover ... and convince them that the only way you can discover it is by doing a bit of real mind reading!

Moving along to the next kind of special magic, you might enjoy including a simple X-ray-eye trick in your next performance.

Our eyes can do many things for us, but we are all also very much aware of the things they can't do. They can't see things too small, too far away, hidden behind walls or when there isn't any light. Because of these last two limitations, X-ray-eye tricks seem almost unbelievable to an audience!

THE BLINDFOLD AND THE BAG

After borrowing a clean pocket handkerchief and folding it in half diagonally, the magician asks that it be tied across his eyes to serve as a blindfold.

When this is done, he gropes around on his table until he finds a paper bag. He asks that this also be dropped over his head to further prevent him from seeing anything. This is done.

A member of the audience is invited to pick up a deck of cards from the table, shuffle them and hand one to the magician. Because he is unable to see, the card must be placed in his hand.

He holds the card up in front of the bag that covers his head as though he were looking right through the bag at it. He says:

'Ah, yes, I am beginning to see a little something. It seems to be the colour red. Is this a red card? Oh, I seem to see hearts and there are ten of them. Is this card the ten of hearts?' It is.

He is handed still another card, and again he 'sees' the card correctly. He continues, correctly, for several more cards.

He then proceeds to do several other experiments to prove

that he can actually look right through the cloth handkerchief and the paper bag.

Finally the handkerchief and bag are removed and anyone who thinks he can 'see through' his trick is welcome to try them on but he will always be left 'in the dark'.

HOW TO DO IT: Perhaps the most surprising thing about this trick is why you can safely allow the audience to try on the bag and blindfold. They will not be able to see through them because it is impossible ... in fact, you can't either! To see through it, you would really need X-ray eyes, and if you had those you wouldn't be bothering to read this, would you? You don't see through it ... but you do see *under* it.

You will probably have actually to try this to convince yourself that it will work easily. To do it, first find a man's large white handkerchief and a paper bag that fits loosely over your head (use a paper bag – never a plastic bag!). You will also need a deck of cards. None of these requires any preparation.

Lay the handkerchief flat on a table and fold one corner across diagonally to meet the opposite one. This produces a double thick triangle. Hold each corner in your hands and tie it behind your head so it covers your eyes like a blindfold. (In your performance you would borrow a handkerchief, and allow a helper to tie it.)

You will not be able to see if you look straight ahead which is the way you usually look. Now, shift your eyes downwards and you will discover that you can see your waist and feet clearly! Practice keeping your head up and rolling your eyes down. This will look as though you are actually staring forward.

Now drop the paper bag over your head while keeping your head straight up. Your nose will push the paper away from your face and you will still have a clear view down. To the audience, it now appears that your eyes are completely blacked out.

Pick up the cards from the table. If you have to grope for them this is fine. Remember that you must appear completely blinded. Finally, in fact, it is wise to ask someone to find the cards for you, shuffle them, and hand you any one.

Hold your hand close to your waist as you take the card. Turn it over several times when you get it, and by rolling your eyes down, you will be able to see the card clearly. Finally, hold it up before your face and name it. Repeat this several times with other cards. You will have to be an actor ... seeing the card at your waist ... convincing your audience that you actually see it when it is in front of your face. This is the real secret of this trick!

You will probably want to do several more quick tricks to further convince the audience that you can actually see through the coverings. Naturally you must restrict yourself to things which can be done by seeing objects close to your waist or feet. Perhaps you can invent some ideas of your own?

As unusual as X-ray eyes may seem, this kind of special magic is not as odd as the work of escapologists. These amazing magicians enjoy being sealed in a box which is weighted and dropped into a river, or being tied in a straight jacket and making their escape while hanging over the edge of a twenty-storey building from a rope tied to their ankles. To be a successful escapologist requires many years of practice and experience. Every magician who is just learning, however, can include an escape trick in his 'bag of tricks'. This will make his performance much more fun for his friends and for himself.

FIFTY FEET OF ROPE

The escapologist hands a fifty-foot coil of rope to a group of spectators and invites them to use it all to tie him up. Before they begin, however, he hands one spectator a watch and asks him to determine how long it takes the assistants to tie him using all of the rope.

Once he is securely tied he steps into another room and asks the helper with the watch to time his escape.

In less time than it took to tie him the escapologist steps out completely free holding the rope all knotted and tangled in his hands.

HOW TO DO IT: Probably this trick sounds wonderfully exciting and it certainly can be, but it will not work itself . . . you are going to have to work fast and hard and make it work.

The secret is simple: it is practically impossible to tie a person tightly using fifty feet of rope! You can count on the fact that the rope will provide you with plenty of slack for 'working room'. But, some other facts also help to make it easy:

Begin by handing one end of the rope to an assistant. Hold your hand out and ask him to tie the rope to it. Be sure he uses simple overhand knots to do his tying. With only one free end to work with, the knot he ties *will* be a *slip knot* which can be easily pulled open. The easiest way to understand this is actually to try it.

The only knot which can be tied at the end of a rope that will not slip is a bowline. To avoid this be sure your assistant uses only simple overhand knots for all his tying.

There is an old saying: 'Too many cooks spoil the broth.' This is important here also. Invite lots of people to help with the tying. Each person will have his own ideas about how best to tie you, so, in effect, each person is competing against the others and you can be assured of a very sloppy job.

Fifty feet of rope is an awful lot of rope. Perhaps your helpers start off with good knots and pull the rope tight, but they will soon tire of this. To make the job faster they will finally begin simply to wrap the rope around your arms and body. (Keep your feet free so you can walk into the next room.) Once they begin just wrapping the rope you will look very well tied, but they will be leaving you a lot of slack you can throw off quickly later.

All of these facts will work together in your favour. The extra rope will allow you to pull and tug until you can free the hand that was first tied (with the slip knot). This is the real secret of escaping: *get one hand free* and forget about trying anything else until you do! It's much easier than it sounds.

Once the hand is free you can use that hand, plus all the slack to remove the rope. Untie only the knots you must untie, as you will find most knots don't really do much anyway.

With a little practice you will find it is quite easy to beat the time it took to tie you. Your helpers spend considerable time being sure you are carefully tied, but you really don't care what kind of a mess you make of the rope in getting free.

Like all of the special magicians mentioned in this chapter, the escape artist must work hard and know just what he is doing. The kinds of tricks these magicians perform are so different from ordinary magic, so it is very rewarding for the beginner to include one or two of them in his 'bag of tricks.'

CHAPTER 12

NOW, ON WITH THE SHOW

The telephone rings. Someone wants to speak to Jim. Somebody has heard that Jim is a magician and wants him to do some tricks for a party. Perhaps he has done this before . . . but suppose this is his first request.

Every magician begins to learn his trade by showing, to his parents and friends, those tricks he most enjoys. Perhaps he brings a few to school or to a friend's birthday party. He begins to realize how easy it is to fool people and to entertain an audience. More important though, people no longer know him as just Jim Brown; they begin to call him Jim the Magician! And maybe it isn't long before Jim makes up his own name and begins to call himself, Alfonso the Mysterious, or Merlin the Magical.

People have discovered that it is fun to have him around. He can do things that others can't do. His reputation spreads. Finally, he receives a telephone call from someone who wants him to perform in front of an audience he doesn't know!

What does he do? First, he agrees to do the show. If he doesn't agree then he really doesn't want to be a magician. Reading a book and learning some tricks is only part of it. Magic must be performed in front of real people, and many rules must be learned and memorized. The rules in this book were discovered by magicians who have done their acts for real audiences. Here are some of them:

The audience enjoys magic because it is fun. The magician must be having fun along with them.

The magician is just a special kind of actor. An actor's job is to entertain his audience. A piece of rope can't entertain an audience, but the magician holding the rope can!

Use a variety of the 'tools of your trade': vanishes, appearances, penetrations, etc. Don't repeat the same kinds of tricks.

Don't try to be myterious. Nobody will believe you can really do magic. Use lots of comedy tricks.

A magician is wise to think about these rules as he plans for his magic show. Perhaps you should think about these rules. One day you might get a phone call and you'll want to be ready. That is, of course, if you have decided that you really do want to be a magician. The plan for a good show could simply be called ONE, TWO, THREE, and GO. Here's how it works.

ONE ...

Decide what kinds of tricks you will do. Three questions you should ask on the phone will help you decide.

1 How big will the audience be? Use the right *size* tricks.
2 What will be the ages of the audience? If it is a party for twelve-year-olds, choose appropriate tricks for them. If it has mixed ages, try to choose something for all ages but mostly do tricks that the *youngest* people will understand and enjoy.
3 How long a show will you do? NEVER do a show longer than a half hour. Try to suggest 15 or 20 minutes. Remember the old show rule, 'always leave your audience wanting more'.

With these facts you are ready for *programming* or arranging the tricks you have selected in a pleasing order. To do this be sure you have a good variety and have included many tricks you are really comfortable doing.

TWO ...

Setting your act. Setting is another word for programming. You must arrange your tricks in an order that will keep the audience interested and waiting to see what will come next.

There is no magic formula for doing this. Every magician has his favourite arrangement. Here are some suggestions that might help you decide on yours:

Make your first trick special. It should be one you know well. Select one that will 'prove' that you are a magician and will 'promise' more entertainment.

Follow this with a longer or more complicated trick or two while your audience is alert and interested.

Follow this with a couple of quick tricks. Use plenty of comedy.

Alternate long and short tricks. Be sure that you use different kinds of tricks. Don't, for example, do two vanishes in a row.

Choose your final trick carefully and leave your audience happy. Make the last trick very funny or choose one that is very surprising. If people applaud you can simply say, 'Thank you' and walk away, but young people often do not applaud. Be prepared to say something so they will know you are through. You might try. 'And that's my magic show for today. I hope you enjoyed it and that I succeeded in fooling you ... just a little.' Or, you might end with a bit of comedy, 'And, as the magician said to the girl he had just cut in half ... it was a real pleasure to have sawed you!' It's corny but it will leave your audience laughing.

As you programme your show, you must also think about how you will move from one trick to another. This has to be done smoothly and will require that you know exactly what you will be doing next. To turn a programme into a show requires practice, and this is step number three.

THREE ...

Practice your programme. Practice means many things. Certainly you should, like all good magicians, try your tricks in front of a mirror; everyone knows magicians do that. But practice means more than this.

Lay out your *entire show* just as you will do it. Have your programme written on a card and arrange the tricks in that order. Rehearse the entire show ... not just the individual tricks, but all of them, one after another, just as you will be doing in the real show.

Practice going from one trick to another. You will discover many unexpected problems. One trick may clutter the table and you might find that it is impossible to do another one right afterwards. A trick may not work, or you may forget part of it. (Magicians usually have an extra one ready for this emergency.)

Where will your helpers stand? Make sure they can't see any of your secrets. Where do you put things when you've finished with them? These are just a few of the many problems you should think about when you practice your whole show. Actors always do this; it is called a dress rehearsal.

Rehearse what you are going to say. Often this is more important than the tricks themselves. Practice 'talking your show aloud' as you do the tricks. Learn how much time you have to talk.

Remember not to use words which won't mean anything to your audience, such as 'silks' instead of handkerchiefs. And please don't start each trick by saying 'Now, for my next trick ...' or 'Now I'm going to do ...' Imagine yourself sitting in the audience ... what would you like to hear?

Saying and doing the right things at the right time to get the most entertainment from your show is called *timing*. A person who practices his timing, his mis-direction, and his tricks is called a *showman*. The best magicians are also the best showmen, and this requires a great deal of hard work.

GO ...

The day has come for the new magician to head out to his first real show. This is called *playing the date*.

All your materials should be carefully packed in a suit-case. Be certain you have everything. Most homes do not have a supply of magical apparatus.

Try to arrange your tricks in order in the suitcase. At least keep all the necessary equipment together for each trick.

When you arrive, have a table set up where you can perform. It is wise to ask that it be placed in a corner of the room so nobody can sit behind you or directly beside you either. You don't want your audience to see some of your secrets, but more important, they probably won't be able to see the things they should.

If possible, ask that no one be in the room while you set up and get ready. If this can't be done, ask an adult to keep children away while you set up your equipment on the table. Your suitcase will allow you to do this nicely. Open it away from the audience and reach behind the cover to adjust your gimmicks and prepare the tricks.

Now ... you're on. You've been introduced as Jim the Magician ... and everybody is looking at you. Your hands will be shaking, your knees will be knocking, and you'll feel a bit sick to your stomach and faint in the head. Don't worry about these symptoms, every actor has them. They are called 'butterflies in the stomach', 'opening night jitters', or 'stage-fright' ... and they have the most amazing way of disappearing once you have surprised your audience with your first trick.

Finally, you may discover still another surprising sickness following your first real magic show. People will be telling you how much they enjoyed it and how anxious they are to have you back ... suddenly you will feel a warm glow all over your body. Your head will be very light, you can talk better than you ever have before, and every muscle in your body is so relaxed it feels like you are floating in air.

Don't be at all worried or concerned about this new feeling. You will feel it after every show you do. I think it is called being 'stage struck' and, more than anything else, it will make you very glad that you wanted to become a magician!